Aurea Vidyā Collection*

——— 20 ———

* For a complete list of titles see page 191.

This book was originally published in Italian as *Cinque Upaniṣad* by Associazione Ecoculturale Parmenides (formerly Edizioni Āśram Vidyā), Rome, Italy.

First Published in English in 2018 by
Aurea Vidyā
39 West 88th Street
New York, NY 10024



ISBN 978-1-931406-26-0
Library of Congress Control Number 2018940676

Cover: *A lady picking flowers*. Punjab Hills (Guler), c. 1800. 'Indian Miniatures' by Silvana Editoriale d'Arte. Milan, Italy.

# FIVE *UPANIṢADS*

*Īśa Kaivalya Sarvasāra Amṛtabindu Atharvaśira*

by

Raphael

(Āśram Vidyā Order)

AUREA VIDYĀ

*Oṁ*. That is Fullness this is fullness
Fullness derives from Fullness
Drawing fullness from Fullness
What remains is still Fullness
*Oṁ śāntiḥ śāntiḥ śāntiḥ*

*Īśa Upaniṣad Invocation*

TABLE OF CONTENTS


| | |
|---|---|
| Notes to the Text | 11 |
| Foreword | 15 |
| *Īśa Upaniṣad* | 17 |
| *Kaivalya Upaniṣads* | 39 |
| *Sarvasāra Upaniṣad* | 59 |
| *Amṛtabindu Upaniṣad* | 81 |
| *Atharvaśira Upaniṣad* | 107 |
| Sanskrit Text | 133 |
| Appendix<br>*Structure of the Śruti and of the Smṛti* | 151 |
| Glossary | 161 |
| Raphael: Unity of Tradition | 187 |

## NOTES TO THE TEXT

### The English Text

1. Square brackets [ ] are ours. They enclose terms and phrases that are understood in the text, as well as supplementary material that is considered helpful for a better understanding of the work.
2. Round brackets ( ) enclose the original Sanskrit of words and phrases in the Five Upaniṣads; translation into English of Sanskrit terms: short explanatory phrases.
3. Double inverted commas ' ' enclose quotations from particular scriptural sources, while single inverted commas ' ' indicate speech within quotations.
4. Except for proper names of people and locations, roman type is used for Sanskrit words (Brahman, Ātman, Hiraṇyagarbha, māya, etc.) in the *sūtras*, which otherwise appear in italic type. Italic type is also used for the English terms of particular interest in a given context.
5. The same noun will have an upper-case initial if it refers to a divine Form (*Vāyu*) and a lower-case initial if it refers to an element or form (*vāyu*).
6. Any discrepancies relating to scriptural references arise from the lack of uniformity in different editions and the different ways of dividing the texts from which they have been drawn.

## The Sanskrit Text

1. The transliteration of the Sanskrit text from the original *devanāgarī* follows the currently accepted criteria and, apart from a few exceptions, does not separate the words.

2. References to verses in the *Upaniṣads* and other texts are given in accordance with the traditional numbering system used in the texts, such as *Muṇḍaka Upaniṣad* II.II.8-9.

## *The Phonetic Formation of the Letters*

According to their mouthpositions

| | | gutturals | palatals | cerebrals | dentals | labials | |
|---|---|---|---|---|---|---|---|
| Simple breathing (formless sound) | h | | | | | | |
| Release of breath | ḥ | | | | | | |
| *Vowels* | | | | | | | |
| short | | a | i | ṛ | ḷ | u | |
| long | | ā | ī | ṝ | ḹ | ū | |
| | | (a) | | | | | |
| *Diphtongs* | | e-ai | | o-au | | | |
| | | | (i) | | | (u) | |
| *Semi-vowels* | | | y | r | l | v | |
| *Consonants* | | | | | | | |
| unvoiced | | k | c | ṭ | t | p | |
| aspirated unvoiced | | kh | ch | ṭh | th | ph | |
| voiced | | g | j | ḍ | d | b | |
| aspirated voiced | | gh | jh | ḍh | dh | bh | |
| nasals | | ṅ | ñ | ṇ | n | m | |
| Sibilants | | | ś | ṣ | s | | |
| Pure nasal sound | | | | | | | ṁ |
| Nasal sound conformable to the consonant | | | | | | | ṃ |

## *Guide to Pronunciation.*

| | | |
|---|---|---|
| a | = | s**u**n |
| ā | = | f**a**ther |
| i | = | **i**f |
| ī | = | f**ee**t |
| u | = | p**u**t |
| ū | = | m**oo**n |
| ṛ | = | **ri**ng |
| ḷ | = | reve**lry** |
| e | = | **a**che |
| ai | = | m**i**ne |
| o | = | h**o**me |
| au | = | l**ou**d |
| k | = | **k**ite |
| kh | = | bloc**kh**ead |
| g | = | **g**ate |
| gh | = | lo**g-h**ut |
| ṅ | = | si**ng** |
| c | = | **ch**alk |
| ch | = | coa**ch-h**ouse |
| j | = | **j**ug |
| jh | = | he**dgeh**og |
| ñ | = | fri**ng**e |
| ṭ | = | dar**t*** |
| ṭh | = | car**th**orse* |
| ḍ | = | or**d**er* |
| ḍh | = | har**d-h**eaded* |
| ṇ | = | cor**n*** |
| t | = | **t**able |
| th | = | an**t-h**ill |
| d | = | **d**ay |
| dh | = | go**d-h**ead |
| n | = | **n**o |
| p | = | **p**ure |
| ph | = | loo**p-h**ole |
| b | = | **b**aby |
| bh | = | a**bh**or |
| m | = | **m**other |
| y | = | **y**ellow |
| r | = | **r**ed |
| l | = | **l**ady |
| v | = | **w**in |
| ś | = | **sh**all |
| ṣ | = | mar**sh*** |
| s | = | **s**at |
| h | = | **h**eaven |
| ṁ | = | b**on**b**on** |
| ḥ | = | aa**h** |

* With the tip of the tongue raised to the roof of the mouth.

## FOREWORD

The *Upaniṣads* are an integral part of *Vedas*, they represent a branch of the primordial Tradition and constitute the essence of *Vedānta* itself. The expression *Vedānta* (end of the *Vedas*) should be understood in the double meaning of 'conclusion', as the *Upaniṣads* are the last part of the Vedic texts, and of 'purpose', because what is being taught is the ultimate goal of Traditional Knowledge.

One can say without exaggeration – writes T.M.P. Mahadevan – that the *Upaniṣads* are the main source of Indian thought and culture. In fact, they have inspired not only the orthodox schools of Indian philosophy, but also some of the so-called heterodox schools, such as those of Buddhism.

The central theme of the *Upaniṣads* is the quest for the Ultimate Reality, they therefore represent Metaphysics in its real sense. This type of research is not an end to itself, for the *Upaniṣads* represent ways of contact and tools of realization; to this end, they indicate a concise and complete sequence that concedes little or nothing the analytical mind.

There are five *Upaniṣads* presented in this text.

The *Īśa* is one of the oldest *Upaniṣads*. Its simple and masterful language has not failed to arouse commentaries, exegesis and doctrinal ideas. In it Śaṅkara, the codifier of the *Advaita Vedānta*, found the concise formulation of his teaching.

The *Kaivalya* teaches how by means of intuitive discernment (*viveka*) and detachment (*vairāgya*) one attains the state of 'Isolation' (*kaivalya*) or 'total Abstraction' from the world of becoming (*saṁsāra*).

The *Sarvasāra* reflects the fundamental theme of the older *Upaniṣads*. The most ardent philosophical questions that the human mind can formulate are entertained here. The *Sarvasāra* is often cited for its importance.

The *Amṛtabindu* contains a purely metaphysical and resolving teaching that allows the being or *jīva* to recognize its deepest and true nature and to realize the identity with the Absolute or *nirguṇa Brahman*.

The *Atharvaśira*, which is of monistic leaning and therefore Shaiva, contains a dialogue propounding a teaching that presents some very precise sequences for the realizational *opus*.

It should be noted that the five *Upaniṣads* are commented by Raphael extensively, and in this respect we can say that these are unique compared to other editions. This is noteworthy because as the *Upaniṣads* are expressed in their own synthetic language, if one does not have the 'key' to the right understanding, they stay obscure and incomprehensible.

Always in adherence to the text, Raphael frames and broadens all the various points in the context of the traditional *Advaita* (Non-duality) teaching, and thus provides the western mind with the key to the comprehension of their symbolic, figurative, and analogical language.

Aurea Vidyā

# *Īśa Upaniṣad*

# INTRODUCTION

It is recognized that the *Īśa* is one of the most ancient, major *Upaniṣads*. It belongs to Chapter XIV of the 'white' *Yajur Veda* and falls within the *Mantra* (ritual) part of the same *Veda*. Its date can be traced back to 700 B.C.

The *Upaniṣad* is conceived in five well-delineated themes and represents a very profound synthesis of the *Vedānta*. It would seem as if it is the summary of a more extensive teaching which was given orally.

The simple and masterly language of the *Īśa* has not failed to arouse exegeses and doctrinal cues. Śaṅkara, the Teacher, found in it the concise formulation of his teaching. Others with lesser depth of thought have limited themselves to simple annotations. There is no doubt anyway that the *Upaniṣad* presents difficulties in interpretation.

It begins with an invocation that seems to be an integral part of the text and brings into evidence two fundamental themes of the *Vedānta*: *That* and 'This'. *That* is the ultimate metaphysical Reality. To say *That* is to say *Brahman nirguṇa*, the Uncaused, the Absolute, always identical to itself. All the beings, in their essence, do not differ from *Brahman*, although the latter does not possess form, structure, dimension and properties. The entire universe, in its principial state and its formal development, finds its support in *That*.

In considering manifestation it can be said that it is pervaded by three aspects: Existence (*sat*), Consciousness (*cit*) and Bliss (*ānanda*). There is no form which does not in fact manifest these three aspects: existence, consciousness, and bliss.

*Brahman* is beyond any qualification; it escapes any intellective understanding. It cannot be contained in mental categories, it can neither be the object of any cult nor of any veneration. *Brahman* as it resides in the heart of all individuals is called *ātman*. *That* is Fullness because not even one thing exists without It.

The universe emerges according to a process which is incomprehensible to the finite intellect and in describing it one is generally obliged to recognize an indefinite hierarchy of divine beings: from the primordial Power to the various complex functions and individual forces.

Such a universe, denominated as 'This' to distinguish it from *That/Brahman*, is a synthesis, a *unity* (the human being with its vehicles being an integral part of it) and it balances itself in extremely strict laws which at the same time are not absolute. The unity represents its ontological state.

'That is Fullness, this is fullness
Fullness derives from Fullness
Drawing fullness from Fullness
What remains is still Fullness.'[1]

The innumerable universal forms in whatever dimension they can exist, are the phenomenon/ideas that are born, grow and vanish but the Idea/essence remains as Fullness.

---

[1] *Īśa Upaniṣad Invocation.*

The angst and the worry arise when the entity thinks of being form/body and, due to metaphysical ignorance, tries to hold on to it and to crystallize it, pretending – in other terms – to render eternal that which can never be eternal, as the intrinsic nature of the objects is characterized by instability. Hence the conflict of the entity that sees its desires, its riches, its ideals, its very corruptible body, and its dearest affections, etc., vanish.

Everything is unstable in a universe represented by passing vortices, in a world in which, when one has just finished defining an object, it has already fled to its annihilation.

The invocation places the accent on the universal aspect or totality; the continuation of the *Upaniṣad* on the other hand, is a *research* into the Real in itself. In order to carry out the research, poetic and at times apparently contradictory formulations are used; which is a typical example of the Indian method of approach.

*Ātman* is not a psychological concept or an intellective category, nor does it become impoverished by sensory representations. *Ātman* is a metaphysical Reality.

In the first *sūtra* there is enunciated the principle of the Being as unity, which provides the phenomenal world with being. The latter must be comprehended and contemplated with detachment. What matters is not to annul the experience, but to *comprehend* its cause and its finality.

In the subsequent *sūtras* (4-8) the unity with *Brahman*, whose realization is the aim of human life, is identified. The consciousness of the individual as phenomenon, torn apart and conflicted, can find its completeness and serenity in letting itself be absorbed by the One-without-a-second. The latter is the only Essence, autonomous and primordial; it is the Source of all beings. It (*Brahman*) 'has placed all things in conformity with truth for all times to come.'

It is difficult to comprehend and interpret *sūtras* 9 to 14. In them the accent is placed on the pairs of opposites: knowledge and non-knowledge, becoming and non-becoming, simple rite and meditation on the Powers.

The *Yajur Veda* from which the *Upaniṣad* is derived, contains, for example, an entire series of rites and sacrifices to propitiate the Divinity. For the precise practice of the formulae many *brāhmaṇas* had to study the text in depth in addition to having to possess particular qualities.

The *Upaniṣad* deals with the foundation of the traditional speculation, i.e. that of duality/polarity.

All dualities are limitations and prisons; they are neither real nor not real, it depends on the point of view from which one positions oneself. Beyond any duality Unity exists and behind it is the Substratum from which the ontological and manifesting One emerges.

> 'Two [things] in truth are in the indestructible, in That which transcends *Brahmā*, in the infinite: deeply concealed there lies knowledge and ignorance. Ignorance in truth is destructible, while knowledge in truth is immortal. But That, which governs both knowledge and ignorance, is other [from them].'[1]

With *sūtras* 15 to 18 the reintegration into the Brahmanic archetypal world is actualized.

The Vedic symbols Agni and Sūrya represent the dynamics of this movement of reintegration. At this point the horizons

---

[1] *Śvetāśvatara Upaniṣad* V.1.

are extended to the Infinite and the individuals find their own transfiguration. They are at this point nothing but the very 'face' of the Supreme, of the Witness that shines in omnipotence and omnipresence.

> 'That one who sees Me everywhere [in that universal consciousness,] and everything in Me, nobody can separate that one from Me nor will I separate from him.'[1]

When the sense of ego and the duality have vanished, likewise all conflicts, anxieties, suffering and the angst of waiting, are resolved.

Death itself is won because immortality lives in the without-time. 'This' is nothing but an *appearance*, a phenomenon, the world of names and forms, which vanishes for one who has Awakened to the reality of the *ātman*. *That*, the One-without-a-second, shines, instead, in its absoluteness and unconditioned-ness, since it is its foundation.

R.

---

[1] *Bhavagadgītā* VI.30, by Raphael. Aurea Vidyā. New York.

## *Invocation*

*Oṁ*. That is Fullness, this is fullness
Fullness derives from Fullness
Drawing fullness from Fullness
What remains is still Fullness
*Oṁ śāntiḥ śāntiḥ śāntiḥ*

*Om* is the *mantra* of the supreme *Brahman*.

For *Vedānta* metaphysics, between the name and the object designated with that name there is a precise and non-arbitrary relationship. With the modern scientific discoveries one can comprehend their immense value and their profound importance.

Every form/object is nothing but a combination of electromagnetic vibrations that must necessarily have a precise coloration and a specific sound; so, every vibratory state is at the same time color and sound.

The atom is a rhythm of light and of sound; to know the intimate vibratory combination of the forms means to comprehend their harmonic structure; it could be said, their 'identity card', their name.

*Word* is sound and the *word* of *Brahman* is *Aum*. *Om* (as *Aum* is pronounced) is the sound of power par excellence and to know how to resound it means to enter into perfect tune with *Brahman*.

*That*: refers to the absolute Reality, to *Brahman* without a second, which is beyond time/space/causality. Its unconditioned-ness is not touched in the least by the world of names and forms, which represent just simple modifications, shadows on the unqualified screen.

> 'This being is not born and does not die, it did not come into being from anything, nor did anyone [come into being from It.] It is non-born, eternal, always identical and ancient; it is not destroyed when the body is destroyed.'[1]

*Brahman*, due to its intrinsic nature, remains unmodified and is always Fullness and *summa pax*, conditions of the true Being that is not born and that does not die.

> 'What does not exist cannot come into being, of being there is no cessation of existence. This ultimate truth is being revealed by those who have seen the essence of things.'[2]

> In the commentary to this *sūtra* Śaṅkara highlights:

> 'Of the non-being (*asat* = not real), i.e. of that which is not [in the absolute], "there is not," it is not given a "coming into existence" (*bhāva*), where the existing (*bhavana*) is the state of that which is (*astitā*), as [occurs] for heat and cold, etc., [which are sensations/effects] with their respective causes [which are the contacts of the senses with the objects.] In truth, although the heat and the cold, etc., together with their causes, are ascertained through valid means of cognitive evidence [such as sensory perception,

---

1 *Kaṭha Upaniṣad* I.II.18.

2 *Bhavagadgītā* II.16. Op. cit.

etc.,] they do not constitute real entities (*vastusat*): in fact each one [of them] is a modifications (*vikāra*), and a modification is destined to cease (*vyabhicarati*) [therefore it has not the nature of "that which is."]
As for the presence of a pot, etc., (the form), although it is ascertained through sight, is not real in that it cannot be perceived separately from the clay (its substratum), so any modification is not real as it cannot be perceived separately from its cause. Furthermore, not only the effect, as a pot, etc., has no real (*asattva*) nature – as it is not perceived either before its production nor after its destruction – but, also the [substantial] cause [is not real], like the clay, etc., because it cannot be perceived separately from its own cause [i.e. its elemental components, being these an effect, and so on].'

*Brahman* is Fullness because it does not depend on any modification, nor does the modification have its own substantial reality opposed to *That*.

'This' refers to that which we call the manifest world characterized by the six qualities: emergence, empirical existence, growth, maturity, sickness or decline, and death (considered naturally from the empirical point of view).

Such a world is not real (absolute). The universe is simply a modification of the *Mahat*, the Great, the cosmic Intelligence in that principle of the development of manifestation. On the screen of the Being appears the chiaroscuro whose images represent 'This', the manifest or phenomenal appearance. This is not pure illusion or hallucination, just as the dream of the nightly sleeper is not illusion or hallucination; it is only when we compare it with the Unconditioned that it becomes devoid of any value.

# I

*1. The Lord permeates everything in motion in the universal movement. Realize your joy in detachment. Do not desire the goods of anyone.*

The Lord is *Īśa*, or principial *Jīva*, which, being also the One, permeates the entire world. The One contains in itself the entire series of the numbers, it gives the beginning to all things and underlies the indefinite combination of the multiple, without, on the other hand, losing its intrinsic nature of unity.

To attain the Identity with the One it is first necessary to detach from the multiplicity or, better still, to 'comprehend it', and 'integrate it.' Desire is something that drives one out of oneself, and once one has moved out of oneself, one's Identity is lost. Detachment must be considered as the dis-identification from that which *one is not*.

According to the Islamic esoteric teaching the conquest of Unity entails three stages:

1. Science of the Certainty
2. Conquest of the Certainty
3. Perfect Certainty

The first stage is attainable by means of the exoteric teaching, and the focal center of the approach is still the individualized empirical sensation/perception.

The second stage entails the recognition of certainty by means of the direct supra-conscious 'vision.' Here we are in the domain of certain initiations. From the indirect empirical certainty of the first stage we arrive here at a direct 'vision' of the Truth.

The third stage represents the Identity with the One.

*2. Accomplishing the [prescribed]* karman *one can desire to live a hundred years in the world. In this way one is free from error; the individual [though] should not be a slave of the* karman.

If one wants to be long-lived, it is necessary to practice the *karman*, i.e. the Vedic Sacrifice, with great assiduity. The *karman* is the ritual action prescribed by the Vedic texts. Subsequently this word was transposed to a psychological level, acquiring the meaning of recompense of a moral order. Although the individual must follow the Vedic ritual, nonetheless he should not identify with it; in conclusion he must not become a slave of the simple ritual act. The ritual, as any external 'action', must just constitute a stimulating instrument of ascent. To mistake the means for the end is the characteristic of many devotional seekers.

## II

*3. Certainly the universes of a non-divine nature are inter-penetrated by a blinding darkness and in them go, after their death, those who have forgotten their own* ātmā.

When, during life at the gross physical level, the individual has been completely interested in mundane questions without having subjugated his internal powers, at his death he goes to live in those worlds which naturally are not divine. In other terms, his gross vibratory state leads him to dwell in spheres which are adequate to his condition. Everything is regulated by vibratory and gravitational processes; each one is attracted by the consciential sphere of what responds to their internal 'vibrating.'

According to *Vedānta*, everyone creates for himself hell or heaven – just to use religious terms – and self-determines his own rebirth or his own Liberation. Everyone is the forger of his own destiny.

## III

*4. One* (eka)*, immobile and faster than thought in its proceeding. The Gods [themselves] cannot reach It. Although immobile, it overtakes all the others which are in movement. In It Mātariśvan established its own waters.*

The *ātman* is without change, is the absolute Reality always identical to itself, in It any translational movement is already accomplished, therefore there cannot be becoming. The existent is inferior to the *ātman* which is beyond time. Only one who has transcended becoming has consequently transcended his own weaving represented by the *guṇas*. The *jīva* is of the nature of the *Brahman*.[1]

---

[1] Cf. Bādarāyana, *Brahmasūtra* IV.IV.4, by Raphael. Aurea Vidyā, New York.

It is necessary to consider that the teaching of the *Vedānta*, or of the *Upaniṣads*, is of a metaphysical order and its goal is Knowledge and the unveiling of the prime Principles, the realization of the ultimate Truth. This constitutes *paravidyā*.

Mātariśvan, the Vedic epithet of Vāyu, the God of wind and of movement, is the cosmic *prāṇa* from which the entire manifestation arises, it is the 'Materia Prima' which can be assimilated to *prakṛti*; it represents the stimulus (*pra*) to produce (*kṛti*), and therefore it is continuous movement.

*5. It [*ātman*] moves and does not move, it is far although close, it is internal to everything, it is [also] external to everything.*

The *ātman* is the 'Ray of light' which extends to the *jīva* (spiritual Soul) on the intelligible plane and this one, in its turn, gives life to all the bodies/vehicles of the individualized entity. Thus the *jīva* presides over all the bodies/sheaths (*deha* or *śarīra*), from the gross/physical (*sthūlaśharīra*) to that of the *ānanda*. The *jīvātman* resides in the 'Cavity of the Heart' of every existent [being] and represents the immobile (and therefore immortal) Center whose nature is that of the supreme *Brahman*.

The bodies of manifestation are of the nature of the *prakṛti* (= substance, 'matter'), and therefore are corruptible, while the *jīvātman*, as was said earlier, is of the same nature as *Brahman*.

> 'It becomes [transparent as] water, one, the witness, and without duality. This is the world of *Brahman*, or sovereign.'[1]

---

[1] *Bṛhadāraṇyaka Upaniṣad* IV.III.32.

6. *Now, who beholds all the beings in the* ātman *and the* ātman *in all the beings, from It [*ātman*] that one no longer separates.*

The unity of the *ātman* remains behind the mirage of names and forms; the one, who throughout multiplicity has the eye of vision, can always see Unity, and this is *perfect Completeness* or *Fullness.* This implies that by integrating the 'Second' only Unity remains.

7. *Which illusion or affliction can touch he who sees the unity, he whose* ātmā *has become all the beings?*

Only the one whose empirical ego is resolved (as the dream is upon waking) realizes the supra-ontological state of the *ātman* devoid of parts, and can be free from *avidyā* and *māyā* and from its fruits: the transmigration of *saṁsāra.*

> 'When the seer sees the golden Form (*rukmavarṇa*), the *Puruṣa* who is the creator, the Lord and the source which is *Brahman,* then the knower, having shaken off merit and demerit and having freed himself from any contact, reaches the supreme identity.'[1]

8. *He [*ātman*] includes everything; resplendent, incorporeal, devoid of defects, without organs, pure and free from evil, Prophet [*Vate*], regulator of the mind [pure Intelligence], all-pervasive, self-existent, has ordered all things in conformity with truth for all of the time to come.*

---

[1] *Muṇḍaka Upaniṣad* III.I.3.

*Ātman*/Bra*hman* permeates the all as Essence without being touched or impaired, though, as it is its foundation.

> 'This is the truth: as from a blazing and sparkling [fire] a thousand sparks emanate of [its] same nature, likewise my dear, from the Imperishable multiple existences are generated and to the same Imperishable they go and are reabsorbed.'[1]

## IV

*9. They entangle themselves in blind obscurity, those who let themselves be guided by non-knowledge. But those who are attracted by knowledge are entangled in deeper obscurity.*

Those who are guided by the knowledge of rites or *karman* will go and dwell in the world of the ancestors and those who follow the knowledge/meditation on the Divinities will go to the celestial world; these are the two ways: *pitṛyāna* and *devayāna*. The awakened transcends both consciential states.

True Liberation is obtained when every translational movement towards the subject/object has ceased.

It is well to keep in mind that this *Upaniṣad* attributes to the concept of 'non-knowledge' the meaning of simple ritual action – worship of the ancestors, etc., which are the characteristic of the common person – and to the concept of 'knowledge' the meaning of meditation on the Divinities/powers, or *devas*.

> '... The world of the Gods [is attained] by means of knowledge.'[2]

---

[1] *Ibid.* II.I.1.

[2] *Bṛhadāraṇyaka Upaniṣad* I.V.16.

Beyond ignorance and knowledge itself the One-without-a-second exists; beyond duality is the unconditioned *Brahman*.

*10. One thing is the result of knowledge, another thing is that of non-knowledge. This we have heard from the mouths of the Sages.*

*11. In effect, that one who knows these two [ways,] knowledge and non-knowledge, overtakes death by means of non-knowledge and at the same time reaches immortality by means of knowledge.*

The one who attains immortality cannot be said to have reached the integral liberation. The one who is liberated from *karma* can reach *immortality* in a higher subtle world until the *pralaya* or formal cosmic dissolution, thus remaining no longer conditioned by rebirth on the sensible plane; this, though, still implies remaining in the manifest.

The integral liberation is the return to the non-manifest Principle, therefore one realizes *kaivalya*.

> 'Returning is the aim of the Tao,
> Yielding is the way of the Tao,
> All things in the world originated from Being
> And Being originated from Non-Being.'[1]

*12. Those who worship the unmanifest (*asaṁbhūtim*) enter the blind obscurities; those who are devoted to the manifest enter greater obscurities.*

---

[1] Lao-Tze, *Tao-Tê-King* 40.

*13. One thing is the result of becoming [or the manifest] another thing is that of the non-becoming. We have learned this from the mouth of the Sages.*

According to the interpretation of Śaṅkara, *saṁbhūti*, translated as becoming (or manifested), represents the manifesting aspect of *Brahmā*, the universal Soul, *Hiraṇyagarbha*: the golden Germ. *Asaṁbhūti*, translated as non-becoming (or unmanifest) represents the pre-genetic energetic nature, the *mụlaprakṛti* or primordial Cause, the essential base of all living forms. These are always dual aspects of the manifestation, in any case extraneous from the uncaused Absolute. Thus, the *Upaniṣad* invites one to leave the world of becoming and to sever the very roots of the manifest, i.e. of *māyā*, which are to be found in the causal body of the great Lord of the Life (the ontological state, which would be the One-many of Plato). Only *Brahman* devoid of time, space, and causality exists, free from any event/process/conflict; it is in It that one needs to immerse oneself; It corresponds to the One-Good of Plato, or to the One of Plotinus, or to the Being of Parmenides.

*14. In fact, one who knows these two: manifestation (*saṁbhūtim*) and dissolution (*vināśam*) is freed from death through dissolution and obtains (*aśnute*) immortality by means of becoming (*saṁbhūtyāmṛtam*).*

All the universal effort tends towards *pralaya*, the absorption into the causal Principle after the period of extroversion. The knowledge of the 'cosmic Breath' leads to the awareness of the fundamental polarity of quiet or equilibrium and of movement by means of which one attains the integration of all polarities, the 'end of the journey.' What is important is to awaken to this awareness.

*15. The face of the Truth is concealed by a golden disc. O Pūṣan, take away [the latter] so that the one who is [already]* satya *may* dṛṣṭa*: see it (know it).*

Truth resides behind the disc of fire, and Pūṣan, the solar Divinity, is invoked in order that it rends the veil and manifests the ultimate Reality.

*16. O Pūṣan, the one* Ṛṣi, *O Yama, O Sūrya, O Prajāpati, the uncommon splendor, which is your very own nature, I perceive it: I am this all-pervading* puruṣa.

The *Ṛṣis* are the great Sages who have 'seen' the *Vedas* and the *Upaniṣads*.

Yama is the God of death and the first man, the son of the Sun; in the *Kaṭha Upaniṣad* Yama welcomes Naciketas, the disciple, and gives forth the teaching which is liberating. Prajāpati is the Lord of the creatures, the Creator of all the beings.

In the *sūtras* 15 and following, there is brought into evidence the re-integration of the principial worlds, of the conscious spirit or *jīvātman*.

In the Hermetic Teaching it is said: 'I am the same Spirit who dwells within your form...'

*17. The breath [fuses] with the imperishable Air... Here, this body ends up in ashes. Om! O creative Power, remember that which has been accomplished. O creative Power remember, remember that which has been fulfilled.*

The breath of individualized life is reabsorbed in the principle of the universal *prāṇa* and the body, lacking the sacred fire, ends up in ashes. The creative intelligence (*kratu*) is the possibility of performing an action.

*18. O Agni, lead us on the right path, may we obtain the Fullness. O Divinity, you who know all the manifestations, remove the error that leads us astray. We salute you repeatedly with homages.*

*Here ends the Īśa Upaniṣad*

*Kaivalya Upaniṣad*

## INTRODUCTION

The disciple who, by way of ascesis, arrives at the comprehension of the supreme Real, attains the state of *kaivalya*, i.e. of Isolation or integral abstraction. Isolation of course, from that which 'is not' Real.

Patañjali, the codifier of the *Yoga darśana*, devotes the entire fourth book of his *Yogasūtra* to the realization of *kaivalya*. The last three *sūtras* (32.33.34) of the fourth chapter state:

> 'Therefore the [three] *guṇas* having attained their purpose, [in them] the process of the modifications comes to an end.
>
> The change which is related to the moments and which is knowable at the end [of the modifications], is the succession.
>
> *Kaivalya* follows the re-absorption of the *guṇas* [or of the three constitutive elements] because they are devoid of purpose for the *puruṣa*; [there is *kaivalya*] when the consciousness is founded on its very own essence.'[1]

Returning to the *Vedānta*, the only reality is the all-pervading *Brahman*, the One-without-a-second in its *kevala* condition. All the rest is phenomenon that appears and

---

[1] Cf. Patañjali, *The Regal Way to Realization* (*Yogadarśana)*, by Raphael. Aurea Vidyā, New York.

disappears in front of the *Sākṣin*/ Witness which is beyond any phenomenal appearance.

True knowledge is that which is able to unveil the ultimate nature of Reality, which alone can resolve all oppositions, contradictions and polarities.

The *Kaivalya Upaniṣad* teaches that by means of discernment/discrimination, detachment and renunciation of the unreal phenomenal, one obtains the integral liberation or the awakening to what one really is. It belongs to that group of Shivaite *Upaniṣads* of the *Atharva Veda* and therefore, propounds *Śiva,* one of the three aspects of the *Trimūrti,* as inner contemplation.

*Sūtras* 2 to 5 indicate the preliminary conditions and the suitable instruments to transcend Ignorance/*avidyā*.

*Sūtras* 6 to 11 put in front of the 'gaze' of the disciple the divine Essence in its formal condition endowed with attributes, or *saguṇa Brahman*, and the contemplation on the divine image of *Śiva* with the precise pronunciation of the sacred *mantra Om*, the syllable of great efficacy which is able to rend the veil of *māyā*.

*Sūtras* 12 to 14 make known the nature of the *jīva* which spans the three states of waking, dream and deep sleep.

In *sūtras* 15 and following the nature of *nirguṇa Brahman*, devoid of attributes, and the uniqueness of the *ātman/Brahman* are demonstrated, thus the awareness of the disciple about the realization of the Identity with *That* opens up, and therefore the integral liberation from the metaphysical *avidyā*.

R.

*Hari Om*

*1. Āśvalāyana, having approached Parameṣṭhin, the blessed, told him: 'O Blissful, teach me the highest science of* Brahman *(*bramavidyām*), that which the best honor, that which is concealed from the majority of the human beings, in such a way that, without delay and removing any error, I can take back the identity with the supreme* puruṣa.'

We are able to notice how many *Upaniṣads*, *yoga* treatises, or spiritual texts in general, begin with the sacred syllable *Om*. In the sacred Science, sound is of exceptional importance because it creates specific effects on different levels of consciousness. The entire universe is a synthesis of a Sound that responds to the ontological state. *Brahman* is *aśabda*, without sound.

In the *Chāndogya Upaniṣad* we find:

> 'Of these entities the earth is the essence, of the earth water is the essence, of the water the herbs are the essence, of the herbs man is the essence, of man the word is the essence, of the word the *Ṛg* [*Veda*] is the essence, of the *Ṛg* [*Veda*] the *Sāma* [*Veda*] is the essence, of the *Sāma* [*Veda*] the *Udgītha* is the essence.

This, which is the ultimate essence of the essences, is the supreme, it is suitable for the supreme state and is the eighth, it is the *Udgītha*.'[1]

Every kingdom of nature is the result of a particular sound; therefore we have four sounds – if we can express ourselves in such a way – and three supra-physical or ultra-sounds, to use a modern terminology. The four sounds that represent the four kingdoms of nature are the lower notes of the three fundamental sounds.

These seven sounds are resonances of the primal sound *Om* that supports the whole universe and corresponds to white with regard to the solar spectrum. *Om* is the higher octave of the seven sounds. The universal Musician (*Brahmā*) on the keyboard of time and space creates the world of names and forms.

*Om* is the fundamental note of the Reality that vibrates within us and can be perceived when the *inner hearing* has opened up to the universal. It is the transcendental sound of the inner law, the eternal rhythm of all that which occurs, the expression of total necessity and, at the same time, the expression of total freedom. The resonance of *Om*, when it is pronounced with the *heart*, is configured in the movement of the arms that, thrown open, contain all that lives.

In the *Māṇḍūkya Upaniṣad* the syllable *Om* is analyzed in its vocal element: A U M (A and U contract into O, therefore the pronunciation is *Om*) which represent three degrees of consciousness: A, consciousness of waking (*jāgrat*); U, consciousness of dreaming (*svapna*); and M, consciousness of deep sleep (*suṣupti*).

---

[1] *Chāndogya Upaniṣad* I.I.2-3.

Manifestation draws its beginning by way of sound which puts into vibration the dormant primordial substance (*mūlaprakṛti*) in order to start its movement, which, in its turn, produces the light (*Fiat lux*). For the *Śruti*, the primordial sound from which the birth of a *manvantara* begins, is *Om*. This sound propagates on all existential planes. A planet, a star, a galaxy, etc., produce sounds that are not perceivable by the human ear. The birth and even the temporal duration of a planet, a sun, or a solar system, may be determined according to their sound.

*2. Then the great Father told him: '[The Science] is known by way of faith, devotion and yoga meditation. It is not due to actions nor to ancestry* (prajayā) *nor to riches* (dhanena)*, but it is due to the detachment/renunciation* (tyāgena) *that many have gained back immortality.'*

In order to transcend darkness, produced by the *guṇas*, that veil Reality within us, there are needed three preliminary factors:

a. Certainty/Faith

b. Devotion

c. Meditation

Certainty, the fruit of supra-conscious intuition, constitutes the first step of the spiritual path. This certainty transcends reason itself. It is not necessary to demonstrate with words that *we exist*: this is a given, it is a certainty. If our body is relative, then there must exist something else upon which it can depend. If ignorance exists, by necessity knowledge must exist; if bondage exists, obviously liberation must exist. All of which is not a simple sentimental belief but an essential intuitive demonstration.

True knowledge carries faith with it. 'Faith – says Saint Paul – is the *substance* of things hoped for.'[1]

If within us this evidential conviction is not present (faith is an elevated degree of unconscious recognition), and if within us the faith or the assent to our absoluteness and non-conditioning is lacking, how can we move towards liberation or Reintegration?

To have this intuitive certainty means to slowly penetrate into the domain of perfect Peace. The profound recognition of the one existence or of the Intelligence that illuminates everything works miracles, creates events and breaks circumferences. This characteristic, by itself alone, pushes towards the contact with the Infinite and renders the impossible possible.

The true 'water of Life' is *awareness* without beginning and without end.

Certainty about the Way and the devotion to the liberating and freeing Ideal, go hand in hand. The recognition of a treasure brings to life the aspiration and the devotion to conquer it. Wherever that is, the heart leads us towards it with devotion. There is no human being who is not devoted to something, money, professional career, family, office, mundane pleasures, art, science, etc.

The aspiration is the flame that burns all the debris which impede the unveiling of the *ātman*.

Meditation is a powerful tonic that electrifies all the cells, permeating them with resolving vibrations and irradiating them with beneficial influences; it opens the doors of intuitive

---

[1] St Paul, *Letter to the Hebrews* 11:1.

knowledge, it elevates and fortifies the mind and leads the aspirant towards the source of the supreme *ātman*.

Its phases can be summed up as follows: attention, concentration, meditation, contemplation or *samādhi*. They are four phases of a single process.

*Dhyāna*, or meditation, is the means through which one arrives at dominating the senses; it constitutes the means to fix the mental fire on the One, excluding all the sensory objects. Meditation creates the correct accord between the mind and the Principle.

Meditation can be with seed (object of meditation: Christ, Buddha, Śaṅkara, Śiva, or love, joy, life as undivided unity, etc.) or without seed or ideal content. As the *Bhagavadgītā* teaches (chapter XII), meditation on the Non-manifest (without object or seed) is more difficult than that on the manifest.

> '*Śraddhā* is the trusting adherence [faith] to the truth expounded in the Scriptures and by one's own guru; with this one comes to apprehend reality.'
>
> 'High among the means which lead to liberation is devotion. The constant search for one's own real nature is called devotion.'
>
> 'To those who seek liberation, the *Śruti* identifies the principal factors as faith, devotion, and the practice of meditation (*śraddhābhakti dhyāna yoga*). Those who give themselves unceasingly to these free themselves from the slavery of bodies that live under the force of ignorance (*avidyā*).'[1]

---

[1] Śaṅkara, *Vivekacūḍāmaṇi* 25, 31, 46, by Raphael. Aurea Vidyā, New York.

*3-4. The ascetics enter into that which is beyond the firmament, [which lives] concealed in the cave and which remains immensely brilliant; by means of knowledge they comprehend the sense of* Vedānta*; with mental purity and with renunciation they find the liberation which transcends death itself, in the world of* Brahmā *(*brahmaloka*).*[1]

*Sūtras* 3 and 4 enter into the essence of the question: what is the essential and fundamental condition to reintegrate oneself into the Principle?

The resolving force that transcends *avidyā* is not riches nor meritorious actions nor the observance of the simple family code of procreation; rather, it is detachment. Detachment from every pair of polarities: attraction/repulsion, good/evil, finite/infinite, manifest/unmanifest, joy/pain, etc.

Every polarity is nothing but cosmic 'breath' that is born, grows, and transforms itself. Detachment from the dualistic transforming process gradually leads to *Brahmā*. 'Breath' is composed of an inter-conditionality and co-presence of transcendence and immanence, of substantial non-being and being, of process/becoming (as elliptical movement) and of immobility (as movement rotating on itself). Beyond all this formal rainbow only the Substratum or omnipresent and all-pervading foundation exists; Substratum ungraspable by rational logic, which, although it influences every dualistic event, remains as simple Witness. It is *akṣara* (imperishable) and *akartṛ* (non-acting).

---

[1] See, *Muṇḍaka Upaniṣad* III.II.6.

*Saṁsāra* (the world of contingent names and forms) and *nirvāṇa* (the principial a-formal) are two contingent aspects that find in *Brahman* their possibility of being.

> 'The Principle operates as a pole, as the axis of the cosmic aspect of the beings; of it we just affirm that it is the pole, the axis, without trying to explain it... The modifications, effect of a single law, do not alter the immutable all. The opposites find co-existence in this totality, with no self-ruin.'[1]

Those who have been able to detach themselves from death as well as from life itself, place themselves in the incommensurability of the Center of what one is.

The dynamics of detachment implies profound discrimination, retirement from every periphery, comprehension of one's own psycho-physical space, and knowledge of the laws that regulate the correct polar relationship. Detachment is neither abandonment nor unmotivated renunciation, nor inhibition, and even less, flight or evasion. It is necessary to detach oneself from what one is not, to realize that which one is *ab aeternum*.

*5. In a solitary place the ascetic, sitting in a serene attitude with head and back in perfect alignment, being at the last* (anty) *of the* āśramas, *and having brought to silence all the organs of the senses, turned towards his own Teacher with devotion,*

---

[1] *Chuang-Tze* XXV.10.

*6. With the mind in the lotus of the heart (*hṛtpuṇḍarīkam*), free from passion and from pain, pure, freed from identification with the forms, source of* Brahmā *without beginning, nor intermediate, nor end, immortal, one (*eka*), sovereign, essence of intelligence and beatitude (*cidānanda*), without form (*arūpa*), prodigious,*

*7. Supreme Lord, united with [his spouse] Umā, powerful God who possesses three eyes (*trilocanaṁ*), with a blue throat (*nīlākaṇṭha*), this is Him, who represents the matrix of the elements (*bhūtayoni*), the Witness of the totality beyond* tamas *or darkness, the* muni *pacified and in meditation, tries to attain it.*

The *āśramas* (conditions of life) constitute the four stages of life according to the classic modalities of the *Brāhmaṇas*: *brahmacārin* or disciple, *gṛhastha* or head of household, *vānaprastha* or hermit, *saṁnyāsin* or wandering ascetic who has renounced everything.

It is necessary to recognize that one's own Teacher is the *ātman* that dwells in the cave of the heart. Therefore the true Instructor must be the *ātman/Brahman*, then, possibly, come Teachers at the physical or subtle level who obviously are of great help for the disciple.

In this *Upaniṣad* meditation is consecrated to *Śiva*, as supreme Being. Umā represents the spouse of *Śiva*. The supreme Being possesses three eyes that have the nature – symbolically speaking – of the *soma,* of the sun and of the fire. 'God is a fire that consumes.'[1]

---

[1] *Deuteronomy* 4:24.

*Sūtras* 5 to 7 explain the physical and psychological conditions of one who wants to begin transcendental meditation on the One/*Śiva* that contains in itself the entire manifestation, and that dwells in his own heart. The disciple for Realization must meditate thus on the center of the heart or *anāhata cakra*, which is behind the spine at the level of the thymus gland, with the heart devoid of emotion and commensurate with the highest spiritual virtues.

*8. He is* Brahmā, *he is time, he is* Śiva, *Indra, and he is indestructible, supreme and sovereign. In truth He is* Viṣṇu, *he is* prāṇa, *the fire that brings about the destruction of the world; He is the moon (*candra*).*

*9. [He] is the totality, forever present (*bhavya*), eternal (*sanātana*). By knowing Him one goes beyond death: there is no other path to secure Liberation.*

*10. He is the* ātman *which is in all beings, and all beings are in Him; it is by seeing Him that one attains the Identity with the supreme Brahma, there is [in truth] no other means.*

*Sūtras* 8 to 10 demonstrate how, only by permeating ourselves with the principial Essence can we transcend the entire process of change and of conflicting duality. There is no true liberation unless we re-enter this pre-Adamic condition. *Brahman*, the Unconditioned and the Uncaused foundation of the all, can be attained by means of the realization of Unity. We cannot enter the Non-manifest unless we have previously realized the synthesis and the integration of the manifest, i.e. the integration of the Second. *Śiva* represents the Unity that contains in itself all the beings; by welcoming Him in our heart all beings unite in the consciousness of *Śiva*.

It is well to keep in mind the following distinctions of a metaphysical order: *Brahman* or *Brahma* (neutral) constitutes the Unconditioned, the unqualified and undetermined Absolute. Any empirical speculation on its account is futile, whereas, *Śiva/Viṣṇu/Brahmā* constitute the theological Trinity/Unity. *Śiva* represents the synthetic existential will, *Viṣṇu* the intelligence/consciousness and *Brahmā* (masculine) the creative activity.

The *advaita Vedānta* of Śaṅkara primarily utilizes two terms:

*Nirguṇa Brahman* = The Unmanifest without attributes

*Saguṇa Brahman* = The God person with attributes. *Śiva* or *Īśvara*, creator of names and forms.

*Saguṇa Brahman* represents the causal unity that contains in itself the archetypes of the existent, which will develop throughout the ages of manifestation, becoming simple prototypes; only *nirguṇa Brahman*, the One-without-a-second in its non-dual absoluteness coincides with the metaphysical state.

*11. Considering one's own 'I' as a twig to start the sacred fire, and the sacred syllable (*praṇavam*) as another twig, the Sage (*paṇḍita*), by exercising discrimination that unveils Knowledge, succeeds in extinguishing bondage.*[1]

---

[1] Cf. *Śvetāśvatara Upaniṣad* I.14.

The 'I' must constitute a simple twig to be burnt in such a way as to liberate the imprisoned consciousness. *Om* rends the veil of *avidyā*.

When we try to ideate or create a form/image, the 'I' inherent in that form is born. It is the product of a 'precipitate', it is separating out of the One as totality. If the object/anxiety is born in us, we say: 'I am anxious.' When, on the other hand, happiness is born, we say: 'I am happy.' The 'I' of the moment is the product of a reaction, in this case anxiety or happiness.

When the clay from its homogenous condition takes, for instance, the form of a vase, the 'I'/vase is born and this '*I*' believes itself to be absolute, while in truth it is veiled by *māyā* and lives in continuous conflict precisely because it is a simple relative that has birth, growth and death.

All human beings are nothing but indefinite 'I's/vases/ bodies that are born, grow and die swallowed by dualism and by time. As long as there is identification with 'I am this' or 'I am that' there is bewilderment; when the 'I' is transcended, or the part taken back to the All, then there is the condition of absoluteness and of bliss. The *yogi* (*kevalin*) who has realized *kaivalya* has attained the imperturbable peace of the one absolute Essence, without form and without name (therefore it is neither 'this' nor 'that'). This does not imply a loosing of oneself, but a finding of oneself as ultimate Realty. Certainly this awareness of the 'I'/vase/body is no longer, but in its place there is the immortal Reality, the ever-present Substratum, the screen on which ephemeral images/vases/bodies of time and space move. Therefore the *Upaniṣad* invites sacrificing that 'I'/phenomenon that belongs to *saṁsāra*, the source of every travail, and to immerse oneself in the Truth permeated by *sat/cit/ānanda*.

It is inevitable that this teaching, like that of the *Upaniṣads*, is propounded for that one who thirsts for authentic Freedom from duality and from any contingent aspect; therefore, it is not for everyone. Those who are still living with and for the empirical 'I' are not posing themselves the problem which we just addressed. It can be said that their time has not yet come, but sooner or later it will come because the nature of *what one is* cannot be disavowed.

*12. The* ātmā, *having taken the vehicles of the* ānanda *and of the* buddhi *at the universal level, and with its reflection, those of the* manas, kama *and gross physical, is 'darkened' by the* prakṛti *of which the body vehicles are made.*

*13. In the dream state the individualized being enjoys pleasure and pain in a world projected by its own imagination (*māyā*). During deep sleep without dreams, all objects having disappeared, it goes towards a condition of calm [absence of thought].*

*14. Then, under the influence of the actions performed in other existences, this same entity sleeps while awake, having experiences in the three cities. From it is born this beautiful, complete and multifarious thing [which is its world.]*

*Sūtras* 12 to 14 speak of the manifest *jīva*.

Beyond these objectifying conditions (the three cities or the three states of Being) the without form/image, or unconditioned One exists.

Therefore we have:

*Ātman* ⟶ *jīva* {
Gross body (waking)
Subtle body (dreaming)
Causal body (deep sleep)

*15. Support, bliss, and integral consciousness: such is He in which the three cities are reabsorbed. From Him are born the* prāṇa, *the mind, all the sense organs, the sky, the wind, the light and the waters, and the earth that contains all.*

*16. This supreme* Brahman, *universal* ātman, *great dwelling place of the existent, subtler than anything subtle, and eternal, is, in truth, yourself, because 'You [*jīva *are] That.'*

*17. When he who subsists in the waking state, dreaming, deep sleep and in other manifestations, can affirm: 'I myself [as* jīva*] am* Brahman', *he is liberated from all bondage.*

*18. I am distinct from the object of enjoyment, from the subject who enjoys, and from the enjoyment itself; I am the Witness, uniquely made of intelligence, always imperturbable.*

*19. All that exists was born from me, everything is found in me, everything is reabsorbed in me, I [as* jīva*] am the* Brahman *itself without duality (*bramādvayam asmi aham*).*

*Sūtras* 15 to 19 bring back the part to the All, or rather, the phenomenon to the noumenon, the appearance to the Real.

The *jīva,* as a ray of light/awareness of the *ātman*, is reintegrated into the *ātman/Brahman.* After all, this reflection of consciousness is always *Brahman* itself, it just needs to become aware of it. Here is how Plotinus expresses himself:

> 'You [the living one] have already arrived in the All and do not linger anymore in one of its parts and no longer say about yourself: 'How great I am!'; but you leave aside this greatness to become 'all.'
>
> Yet you were 'all' even before; but because you added to yourself something else beyond the all, you, precisely because of this addition, have become small, because the addition did not come from the All – to which nothing can be added! – but rather from the non-all...
>
> Therefore you increase yourself when you throw away the other things, and the All makes himself present to you when you have eliminated them; but to one who stays with the other things, it does not manifest itself. It, on the other hand, has not moved to be near to you, but rather it is you who goes away when It is not present to you. And if you have gone away, you have gone away from It – since It is always present – nor have you gone elsewhere, but, though present, you have turned the other way.'[1]

*20. That which is smaller than an atom is me [as* ātman*], also all that which is large is always me, all that which is present is me, the multiple is me myself. I am the Lord, the*

[1] Plotinus, *Enneads* VI.5.12.

*principial essence, I am like gold, I am the Regulator, and my essence is [made] of bliss.*

*21. I am without hands and without feet* (apāṇipāda)*, of an inconceivable and incomprehensible power. I see without eyes, I hear without ears, and I know because I have discernment. The knowing subject is my very self, I am the knowledge of the* Vedas *and the author of the* Vedānta.

*22. For me [as* ātman*] there exist neither merit or demerit nor death; neither is there birth or body nor organs of the senses or intellect. For me neither earth or water nor fire, wind or sky exist.*

*23. When the supreme* ātman, *which rests in a concealed place, without parts and without duality* (advitīya) *is known, the Witness, exempt from being and from non-being, one attains the pure essence of the* Paramātma.

*Sūtras* 20 to 23 enunciate the aspect of the *Brahman/ ātman*; and we say aspects just for discursive simplicity. The *ātman* has no attributes, nor qualities, these inhere in the *jīva*. At times *Brahman* is mentioned in a negative/positive way: Non-born, Non-being, Non-formal, etc., precisely in order to avoid enunciating it with properties pertaining to the dual manifest condition. *Brahman* is the Substratum of all that which can appear as 'this' or 'that', just as the screen of a movie theater represents the substratum upon which all the images, the events, and the drama of the filmed life appear. Likewise the mental substance represents the substratum of all the images and the pleasurable or un-pleasurable events of the dream. But both the screen and the mind of dream are beyond the forms/events. When the dream disappears, the reflection of consciousness which has given rise to the process of becoming is reabsorbed in the homogenous original Reality.

*Here ends the Kaivalya Upaniṣad*

*Sarvasāra Upaniṣad*

# INTRODUCTION

The *Sarvasāra* is part of the more recent *Upaniṣads* and reflects the fundamental theme of the older ones which, in their turn, constitute the basis of *Vedānta*.

The *Upaniṣad,* which belongs to the black *(kṛṣṇa) Yajur Veda* is based on the *Vedānta* tradition of *Brahman,* of the *ātman,* of the *jīva*, etc., and is often mentioned for its renown and depth of content.

It can be noticed that the text begins by asking the arduous philosophical questions that the human mind has always posited to itself. What are the Absolute, the relative and the link between these two? Who are the experiencer/subject and the object of knowledge? What is *māyā*?

These synthetic concepts are fully developed by the *Vedānta darśana,* to which above all Gauḍapāda and Śaṅkara have made the most valuable contribution. Therefore, although brief, the *Upaniṣad* has the merit of propounding and unveiling the nature of the *Brahman*, of the *ātman,* of the *jīva* and their connections.

The greatest Oriental minds have speculated on the *Vedānta*, above all *advaita* (non-dual), and many Occidental philosophers, as for example Schopenhauer, Berkeley, Bergson, and Hegel himself, even without realizing it, could not do without propounding it in their philosophical formulations.

The *advaita Vedānta* is not exactly monist because this latter word evokes the idea of unity, as quantity, and this necessarily implies plurality.[1] It is a *darśana* that goes beyond any notion of number, any mental concept that rests on any duality. *Brahman* and *ātman* are rigorously equivalent terms, which can interchangeably be used one for the other, because they represent the one Reality, and this Reality for the *Vedānta* is essentially realizational.

One should not think that the *Vedānta* attains a void or emptiness. It is a philosophy which is neither nihilistic nor pessimistic, quite the opposite; it is a philosophy of Bliss and of consciential positivity.

What renders the being a slave is *avidyā*, ignorance concerning the essence of oneself, and therefore of the supra-sensible Reality; that which renders the being free is the Knowledge/*vidyā* (liberation from the *avidyā*).

The entity is the *ātman*, the *ātman* is the *Brahman,* and the *Brahman* is a metaphysical reality imbued with Fullness.

Behind the entire universe of names and forms is the eternal and uncaused Substratum: the supreme *ātman*, and this *ātman* cannot be an *object* of empirical knowledge because otherwise it would not be the ultimate absolute Subject, but one of the many data of perception.

The mind can speculate on all the objective data, but can never speculate on what is the knowing Subject that is behind the mind itself.

'What is that which is eternal and devoid of generation?

And what is that which eternally generates itself and is

---

[1] Cf. *The Path of Non-duality* by Raphael, specifically the chapter 'Non-dualism, dualism and monism.' Aurea Vidyā, New York.

> lacking being? The first one is that which can be known with the *nóesis* by means of *logos* because it eternally remains in the same state. The second, on the contrary, is that which is object of opinion (δόξα) by means of the knowledge of a sensory order, because it is born and perishes and never is (οὐδέποτε) really Being (ὄν).'[1]

And this is also the conclusion of the *advaita Vedānta*: that is, that the supreme Reality is *non-dual* because the second disappears since it has no absolute valence.

We cannot dance on our own shoulders says the Hindu proverb. Therefore, the *ātman* cannot be unveiled with mental analysis because, since it is our deepest Nature, it can only be comprehended with an act of pure awareness. Hence the *Yoga-Vedānta* or *Jñānamārga* (path of cathartic Knowledge), which leads to the fullness of *Brahman*.

The entire universal spectacle is a simple chiaroscuro which is silhouetted on the screen of the infinite *Brahman*. The chiaroscuro, the shadow/light or the indefinite changing, mutable, perishable and discontinuing living images, constitutes the *becoming*, while the screen always identical to itself is the uncaused supreme *Brahman*.

The *Kena Upaniṣad* – which studies the metaphysical aspect of *Brahman*, the foundation of the sacred Science, i.e. of the traditional Knowledge (*jñāna*) – states:

> 'I do not think: I know [the *Brahman*] well; neither that I do not know [it], and [neither that I] know [it]. The one who among us knows this, can neither affirm it nor negate it.

---

[1] Plato, *Timaeus* 27d-28a. (Translation is ours).

To one to whom it is unknown, it is on the other hand known. To someone to whom it [is] known, it is on the other hand unknown. It is unknown to those who [believe that they] know it, while it is known by those who [believe] that they do not know it.'[1]

The *jñānin* recognizes the entire universe in its Essence and its Essence is in identity with the supreme *Brahman*.

R.

---

[1] *Kena Upaniṣad* II.2-3.

What is the nature of bondage (*bandha*)? What is liberation (*mokṣa*), what are knowledge (*vidyā*) and ignorance (*avidyā*)?

What [are] the state of waking, dream, deep sleep and the Fourth (*turīya*)? What are the bodies made of food, *prāṇa*, mind, intellect and bliss?

What are the *jīva*, the category of the five (*pañcavarga*), the knower of the field (*kṣetrajña*), the immutable witness, the internal ruler?

What are the inner *ātmā* (*pratyagātmā*),[1*] the supreme *ātman*[2], and *māyā*?

The inner *ātman* is of the nature of the supreme *ātman*, existent and master of itself.

To consider erroneously oneself just as a simple body, which is not the *ātman*, [means finding oneself] in a constraint.

By eliminating the *vṛttis* (mental productions) one attains liberation.

That which engenders the bonding with the *anātman* is *avidyā*, and that which makes [the bonding] cease is knowledge (*vidyā*).[3]

When the *manas*, through the fourteen sensory organs turned towards the outside and favored by Āditya, perceives the objective forms, like sound, etc., it is [called] the *ātmā* of waking.

---

* The reference numbers are to the Notes at the end of the *Upaniṣad*, starting on page 70.

When one is free from the impressions of the fourteen sensory organs of the waking state, but one perceives directly through the impressions [of the internal organ], like sound, etc., that is [called] *ātmā* of dreaming [or of *taijasa*].

When the fourteen sensory organs are suspended, and therefore there is no cognition of distinction of sound, etc., that is [called] *ātmā* of deep sleep.

When the Witness (*sākṣin*) of the three states, Being, and non-being, is free from the phenomenal process, as Intelligence as such, it is [called] *turīya*.[4]

The energetic whole of the *annakośa* is called the body made of food (*annamayakośa*).

When the fourteen different breaths (*vāyus*) of the *prāṇas*, support the *annamayakośa* they are called *pranamayakośa* (sheath made of *prāṇa*).

When the two sheaths of the *ātmā*, with the fourteen sensory organs, perceive sound and the other properties, one has the *manomayakośa* (sheath made of mind).

When the three sheaths are connected with the [faculty of] discriminating different properties, one has *vijñānamayakośa* (sheath made of intellect).

When the four-fold body produced by non knowledge, as the seed of the fig produces the tree, is connected [to the *ātmā*] one has *ānandamayakośa* (sheath made of bliss).

Perception/knowledge of pleasure/pain resulting from the inner agent, is pleasurable with regard to the object of desire and un-pleasurable with regard to not desired objects.

Sound, touch, form, taste and smell are motives of pleasure and pain.

When – [because of the *guṇas*] meritorious (*punya*) and non-meritorious (*papa*) actions [are produced] – one leaves the body and is connected to another body, that is called *jīva*. [Without the *jīva* the various bodies would be inanimate.][5]

The *manas* [internal organ], *prāṇa*, desire, *sattva*, merit, and all their effects constitute the group of five. He who possesses the group of five, as he does not know the *ātmā*, believes that he is not going to die; this false [belief about] his immortality derives from the closeness of the *ātmā*, of which it represents a limiting condition. It [which possesses the group of five] is called *liṅgaśarīram* [subtle body], the 'knot of the heart' (*hṛdayagranthi*), and the consciousness which manifests in it, is called 'knower of the field.'

It which knows birth and the disappearance of the knowing subject, of knowledge and of the object of knowledge, is called the Witness (*sākṣin*),[6] which is light of itself and is beyond birth and death.

When [the Witness], from *Brahmā*[7] down to an ant, knows the unity operating in the totality of beings it is called the 'Eternal immutable.'

When in differentiation the 'Eternal immutable' appears as the formal existence, similar to a thread (*sūtra*) that supports a string of pearls, it is called the inner *ātmā*.

Truth, knowledge, infinite bliss, free of all limitations, similar to gold with regard to specific bracelets, diadems, etc., are the *ātmā*, which shines in its own essence (*svabhāvātmā*), and which is designated with the word 'you' (*tvam*). Therefore [the *ātmā*] is truth, knowledge/intelligence, infiniteness and of the nature of *Brahma*.*

The Reality does not dissolve.

---

* Cf. *Taittirīya Upaniṣad* II.I.3.

Name, form, time, space and causality dissolve. That which does not perish is the Imperishable.

Knowledge is the name of the inner essence called awareness.

It is called infinite/homogenous that which, similar to the clay in its transformations, the gold in its modifications, or the thread in its compositions [of cloth], precedes the Primordial, and the development of the formal life.

*Ānanda* is that name, similar to the ocean without boundaries, the essence of which is bliss without object.

That one whose object is four-fold, which is beyond the category of name, cause, time and space, is called the constant, *ātmā* [because it is of the same nature as the *Brahman*.]

That which differs both from the term 'you' as subject to limiting conditions, and the term 'that' as subject to subtle limiting conditions, such as the ether whose essence is solely the Reality, that is called supreme *Brahman*.[8]

That which is without beginning but which has an end (*anta*), which is knowledge and non-knowledge, which is real and non-real, which is not [at the same time both] real and non-real, whose characteristic is vacuity, is called *māyā*.[9]

I am not the ego of mundane existence; I am [instead] the Resplendent, therefore the ten organs of sense have ceased.

1. Thus neither the *buddhi* nor the *manas* nor the *ahaṁkāra*[10] (sense of ego) are eternal.

2. [I am] neither the *prāṇa* nor the *manas* nor the *buddhi*, I am totally and forever pure. Eternal (*nitya*) Witness, I am, without doubt (*na saṁśaya*), the state of pure Fullness.

3. I am neither the agent of the action (*kartā*) nor the enjoyer (*bhoktā*); I am the Witness/*sākṣin* of the *prakṛti* and of the forms. My closeness makes the bodies act, giving them intelligence.

4. In the state of eternity, being and bliss, I am pure, made of wisdom (*jñānamaya*). I am, without doubt, the *jīvātman* of all that which exists, the Omnipresent (*vibhu*), the Witness.

5. I am *Brahma* to be known through the entire *Vedānta*. I am not known as the original forms of space (*vyoma*) and 'wind' (*vāta*). I am not form and name, nor action/activity, I am *Brahma* imbued with Being, Intelligence and Fullness.

6. I am not the body; how can birth and death belong to me? I am not the *prāna*; how can hunger and thirst belong to me? I am not the perceptive knowledge; how can pain (*śoka*) and the bewilderment of the mind (*moha*) belong to me? I am not the agent of the action; how can liberation and bondage belong to me?[11]

*Here ends the Sarvasāra Upaniṣad*

NOTES

[1]The *ātmā* appears to be circumscribed by the gross, subtle and causal bodies.

[2]The supreme *ātma* is the unconditioned *ātman*. We can make these two terms more accessible with an example: the air circumscribed by the walls of a vase is the internal *ātmā* while the external air represents the supreme *ātman*. But the air which is inside the vase does not differ from the air which is outside the vase, it is identical.

[3]The *jīva* is that which animates the life of the various bodies of the being in incarnation, both at the individual and the universal levels. See the *Taittirīya Upaniṣad* II.I and following; *Maitry Upaniṣad* II.6 (end of the *śloka*); Plato, *Cratylus* 399d, and also Plotinus, *Enneads* IV.7.9.

The *jīva* is immortal because it is a ray of light/awareness of the *ātman* and therefore of the *Brahman*. Nonetheless it can be darkened or veiled by the qualities of the *guṇas* and therefore it falls into oblivion of that which it really is. The veiling can be resolved by cathartic Knowledge, therefore the veiling is accidental.

The traditional West has the same noetic knowledge: see Parmenides, Plato, Plotinus, Proclus, etc.

To realize this, it is sufficient to consider a single passage of Plotinus; referring to the soul, he writes:

'And yet you were "all" even before; but because you added to yourself something else beyond the all, you, precisely because of this addition, have become small, because the addition did not come from the All – to which nothing can be added – but rather from the non-all. However if someone has made something of themselves through the non-all, he is then non-all, and he will be all once he has eliminated the non-being.

Therefore you enhance yourself when you throw out the other things, and the All makes itself present when you have eliminated them; but for the one who stays with the other things, it does not manifest itself. It, however, has not come to be near to you but it is you who has gone away when It is not present to you.

And if you have gone away, you have not gone away from It – because It is always present – nor have you gone elsewhere, but, though present, you have turned the other way.'[1]

By understanding this passage by Plotinus we can also understand the nature of the *jīva* of the *Vedānta* at the universal level and of the *ahaṁkhāra* at the individual level, because there is identity of vision between them.

[4] Here the *Upaniṣad* deals with the well-known 'states' of the being already formulated in the *Māṇḍūkya Upaniṣad*, masterfully commented on by Gauḍapāda and, in his turn, annotated by the great Śaṅkarācārya.[2]

---

[1] Plotinus, *Enneads* VI.5.12.

[2] Cf. Gauḍapāda, *Māṇḍūkyakārikā*, The Metaphysical Path of Vedānta, by Raphael. Aurea Vidyā, New York.

For a better understanding of the text, we can give some useful indications:

Gross body (*vaiśvānara*): it represents the *jīva* in the waking state (*jāgrat*). Both mind and body are active.

Subtle body (*taijasa*): it represents the *jīva* in the dream state (*svapna*). Only the mind is active.

Causal body (*prājña*): it represents the *jīva* in the deep sleep state (*suṣupti*). Both the body and the mind are at rest, in the latent state.

The five sheaths or instruments of contact with the exterior are:

| | | |
|---|---|---|
| *annamayakośa* | sheath of nourishment | Gross body |
| *pranamayakośa* | sheath of the vital energy | Subtle body |
| *manomayakośa* | sheath of the mind | Subtle body |
| *vijñānamayakośa* | sheath of the intellect | Subtle body |
| *ānandamayakośa* | sheath of fullness | Causal body |

The *antaḥkaraṇa* or internal organ corresponds to the subtle body and comprises: *buddhi, ahaṁkāra, citta* and *manas*.

The *jīva* represents the unitary consciousness; it is the manifested Center around which the vehicles rotate; it is the Soul as a reflection of the *ātman*.

The cosmic correspondences are the following:

| | | |
|---|---|---|
| Gross aspect | = | *Virāṭ* |
| Subtle aspect | = | *Hiraṇyagarbha* |
| Causal aspect | = | *Īśvara* |

*Virāṭ* represents the totality of manifested forms, *Hiraṇyagarbha* the totality of Souls on the subtle plane, while

*Īśvara* represents what we could define as the God person. It (*Īśvara*) comprises the entire field of manifestation, that is to say, the three aspects: gross, subtle and causal, from both the individual point of view and the universal point of view.

Beyond all these degrees of manifestation, and therefore beyond the causal/germinal state itself – within which all the potentials of being are included and not yet manifested (ontological state) – there exists a Foundation that gives raison d'être both to the causal Principle and, consequently, to the entire manifestation. This corresponds, in the vision of Plato, to the One-Good and to the Being as ontological state. The 'Fourth state' is defined in this way by the *Māṇḍūkya Upaniṣad*:

> 'The Sages believe that the Fourth – which has no knowledge neither of the internal (subjective) nor of the external (objective) world, nor simultaneously of the former and the latter, and which, ultimately, is not (even) a unity of integral consciousness as it is neither conscious nor unconscious – is invisible, non-acting, incomprehensible, undefinable, unthinkable, indescribable; it is the only essence of self-knowledge, without any trace of manifestation; it is fullness of peace and bliss without duality: it is the *ātman* and as such it must be known.'[1]

With reference to the three states (*avasthātraya*) of the Being, we can say that the *Vedānta*, along with other *darśanas*, as it wants to discover the integral Truth, takes into consideration the entire experience of the entity. This

[1] Cf. Gauḍapāda, *Māṇḍūkyakārikā*, *Āgama Prakaraṇa*, *sūtra* VII of the *Upaniṣad*, by Raphael. Op. cit.

experience is represented not only by the state of waking, but also by the state of dreaming and of deep sleep without dreams.

When an individual during the dream state experiences certain possibilities of life, it faces some particular experiences, i.e. it is joyful or sorrowful as in the waking state, finds the solutions to problems which it had not been able to resolve in the waking state, or intuits the truth about universal aspects and so on, we cannot not take such a condition of consciousness into consideration.

It is possible to study separately the three states and limit oneself to just consider one portion or a certain aspect of a single state. Let us take, for instance, the experience of the waking state; it can be subdivided into different sections or groups of research: artistic, scientific, philosophical, religious, etc., thus obtaining specific truths that are quite useful, but we have to agree that all this body of knowledge is valid only for the state which we are examining.

It suffices to say that time/space differ in the conditions of waking and dreaming, although they subsist in both cases.

Neither can we maintain in an absolute way that dreaming is a consequence of the subconsciousness of waking, precisely because there takes place in it certain experiences which are outside of the waking framework, as well as there are experienced even events which have yet to happen in the condition of waking.

When we dream, we have the faculty of distinguishing what is real and what is not real, what is pleasurable and what is not pleasurable, which means that waking and dreaming both possess the same perception of reality.

While the dream persists, not only does it offer sensory experiences similar to those of the waking state, but it is considered real by the dreamer himself.

In both these states we find objects and thoughts. We commonly consider *subjective* the objects that we see in the dream, and *objective* those which we perceive in the waking state, and we think that the sensory organs, which in the waking state give us various objective data, are not functioning in the dreaming state.

On the contrary, the sensory organs operate in the dream characters exactly as in the waking state. The subjective and objective possibility exists in both cases. Also when we dream, the senses of touch, smell, sight, etc., are active; some thoughts give us worries, our reasoning functions work normally, we resolve mathematical problems, we reflect on abstract subjects, and we come up with clear and precise solutions. All of this demonstrates that in this condition, both a *tangible and a mental world* exist that are equally distinct as in the waking state: one is objective and one is subjective.

The notion of time and space, although perceived differently, is common to both states. The objects of dream have a certain duration, which is relative to their peculiar condition of existence.

Furthermore, causality exists in both the waking and the dream states.

The objects of dream have their purpose relative to the dream, as those of waking have theirs in relation to the condition of waking.

Riches possessed in dream have certainly no value in the waking state, but also those possessed in the waking state serve no purpose in the dreaming state.

It is obvious that it is necessary to examine the two states independently from one another; thus we cannot study a dream according to the presuppositions and the point of view of the waking state.

The character of a dream content can appear abnormal to us *only* when we gain the waking state back, and not before.

According to *Vedānta* metaphysics, the dreaming and waking modalities constitute a series of perceptions and as such can be reduced to ideas; consequently their universes are equally reducible to a mental construct.

*Advaita Vedānta* develops these themes with rigorous analyses. All of Gauḍapāda's *kārikās* to the *Māṇḍūkya Upaniṣad* refer, as already stated, to the three states of waking, dream and deep sleep without dreams, and also of course to the 'Fourth' or *Turīya*.

5 The *jīva*, as we have already seen, reflects the nature of the *ātman*. It emerges from the 'reaction to contact' with *prakṛti*. With this 'contact' the *jīva* enters into the world of manifestation. Each body on the plane of manifestation presupposes a causal agent which, in its turn, depends on Reality which remains outside of causality. Therefore, we have: form —> *jīva* —> *ātman*. The form is temporal while the *jīva* and the *ātman* are immortal.

6 The Witness (*ātman*) dwells beyond the manifest and therefore beyond the three states that were previously examined. It transcends the knower (*jīva*), the known, and knowledge itself.

> 'The sun does not shine there, nor do the moon or the stars, nor does the lightning bolt. Where is this fire [drawing] from? As it shines, consequently everything else shines, all of this shines because of the splendor of That.'[1]

---

[1] *Śvetāśvatara Upaniṣad* VI.14.

'That which observes all things, but which is observed by none, that which illuminates the *buddhi*, etc., but which is not illumined by it, is the *ātman*. That which permeates this universe, but which cannot be permeated by anyone, that whose light is reflected in the entire universe, shrouding it with its splendor, is the *ātman*.'[1]

[7] *Brahmā* is the idea of the creator God. It is the constructive aspect of the entire world of names and forms, while *Brahman* is totally transcendent, unconditioned, immutable, and always identical to itself. *Brahman* is the Absolute, the foundation in relation to *Brahmā* and what derives from it, while *Brahmā*, or *Īśvara* constitutes the qualified or principial One. In fact, the one who sees the entire manifestation with the eye of *Brahmā* (as the text intends to demonstrate) no longer sees differentiation and multiplicity, but Unity: he sees the many in the One.

[8] Dwelling on it only in a synthetic way, the *Upaniṣad* draws on the well-known upaniṣadic *mantra* '*You are That*' (*Tat tvam asi)*, while in the *Vedānta* texts his *mantra* is conveniently developed from both the philosophical and psychological point of view. In any case the *Vedāntasāra* clarifies how the great aphorism *You are That* must be understood and it explains the meaning of the connection between the visible and the invisible. In the sentence 'this is that Devadatta', the term *this* and *that*, which respectively distinguish the Devadatta of the present time from that of the past, are correlated because they belong to the same Devadatta; likewise in the aphorism *You are That*, which highlights the visible and the invisible, the two terms are correlated by the fact that they refer to the same existential

---

[1] Śaṅkara, *Vivekacūḍāmaṇi* 127-128. Op. cit.

condition.[1] The 'you' and the 'that', which are temporal, are linked to *That* which is immutable and a-temporal.

[9]*Māyā* is that possibility because of which we mistake one thing for another. For example, when a rope is considered to be a snake; this founding error is precisely produced by *māyā*.

T.M.P. Mahadevan writes:

> '*Māyā* can be studied from three different standpoints. The man in the street considers the world of *māyā* to be real (*vistavi*); he who is learned in the Scriptures regards it as unreal (*tuccha*); and the metaphysician who mainly relies on the higher power of his intellect maintains that it is neither real nor unreal (*anirvacanīya*: non-definable).'[2]

These three concepts fuse in the thought of Śaṅkara, who maintains that *māyā* is a phenomenon only in relation to *Brahman,* while for us who live in *māyā* is considered as reality.

If the *ātman/Brahman* constitutes the connective tissue and the sole foundation of the existent, then there must be something that impedes the clear vision of the authentic *ātman*: which is precisely *māyā*.

We consider as real the entire nocturnal universe of dream, we rejoice and suffer depending on the vicissitudes of the dream state; on waking, however, we realize that all of it was nothing but... dream.

---

[1] Cf. *Vedāntasāra* by Sadānanda Sarasvatī, in particular the chapter 'You are That.'

[2] T.M.P. Mahadevan, *The Philosophy of Advaita*. Luzac and Co., London, 1938.

The *Vedānta* brings into evidence that for the Awakened not only the nocturnal universe is a dream/phenomenon, but also that of waking, which is normally considered as real/absolute.

> 'Except through faith, no one has the certainty of being either awake or asleep; as during sleep, one firmly believes oneself to be awake, as is also the case in the waking state. In the dream state one imagines to see space, forms and movements, one feels that time is flowing and that one can measure it, and finally one acts as if one was awake. Therefore half of our life is passed in sleep and, for what is possible for us to understand, we have no foundation that this corresponds to reality, all of our feelings are in fact illusions; but who knows whether this other half of our lives, when we think ourselves to be awake, might not be after all a dream just a little different from the first one, thus making us think of ourselves as being awake while in fact we are sleeping? Just as it happens when we dream that we are dreaming, weaving thus dreams upon dreams.'[1]

[10]The *ahaṁkāra* is the 'sense of ego' or 'that which makes the ego', it is the organ of the sense of ego as individualized entity. These terms, *ahaṁkāra, jīva, antaḥkaraṇa,* subtle body, etc., are at times erroneously mistaken one for the other. It can anyway be pointed out that: the *ahaṁkāra* is the 'sense of ego', which reflects itself in the *manas*, and is the subject; the *antaḥkaraṇa* is the complex of the subtle vehicles which also comprises the *ahaṁkāra*; the *jīva* is the Soul which 'vitalizes' all the body/vehicles of the entity.

---

[1] Pascal, *Thoughts* 456.

[11]The *ātman* is unconditioned and totally outside of time/space/causality. After all, the *ātman* is neither the *jīva*, taken by itself, nor the *antaḥkaraṇa* nor any other vehicle, but it constitutes the essence or the foundation from which all of these possibilities can exist and be.

With its sole presence the *ātman* enlivens everything and everything is reabsorbed into the *ātman* including the *jīva,* as its ray of awareness. To understand this condition, in which on the one hand we have a non-acting Entity that lives in its 'isolated' Reality, and on the other hand a qualified combination of vehicles that determines action/*karma*, we can refer, using it as an analogy, to nuclear atomic phenomenology.

We can offer an explanatory chart about what was said regarding the *ātman*, the *jīva* and the vehicles:

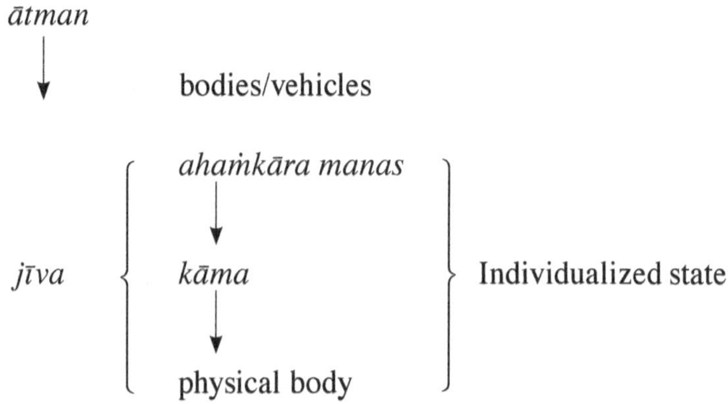


The vehicles/bodies are aleatory, the *jivātman* is eternal since it is of the nature of the supreme *Brahman*.

# *Amṛtabindu Upaniṣad*

## INTRODUCTION

The *Amṛitabindu Upaniṣad* can be placed between the oldest *Upaniṣads* and those from the time of Śaṅkara. It belongs to the *Atharva Veda*. Its teaching propounds the way that allows the *jīva* (soul) to recognize its deepest and true nature and to establish itself as the supreme *nirguṇa Brahman*.

The *yoga* meditation that is presented is constituted by the *mantra Om*, the sound par excellence that is linked to the various states of the principial Being.

After having assimilated the link between the three aspects of the sound *Aum* and the three states of consciousness, both individual and universal, it is necessary to gradually transcend the sound itself, as manifest aspect, and immerse oneself in the *nirvikalpa samādhi* devoid of sound (*aśabdabrahma*).

The *Upaniṣad,* as in fact all the others, presents a concise, synthetic and accomplished sequence. Many *Upaniṣads* (*Kaṭha, Kena,* etc.) diminish, even overtly, the dialectics of the *manas* (empirical mind).

Their concise and esoteric language should not frighten: it is sufficient to be able to interrogate them with attentive perseverance, it is sufficient to *love them* in that truth, it is sufficient to become familiar with their lexicon because they respond with an increasingly clear and penetrating voice.

The *Upaniṣads* form a homogeneous whole in which are grouped, not different doctrines that are divergent or in opposition with one another, but 'intuitive perspectives' that converge into the same vision of Reality. They constitute a robust fulcrum in which the essence of intuitive Hindu speculation is concentrated.

A *traditional* thinker avoids expressing personalized contents of the Doctrine. He wants to be, within the bounds of possibilities, just a faithful vehicle; his effort consists just in the intent to confer a particularly incisive expression to the Doctrine. Therefore, the accent is above all put on effectively transmitting the *message* and not to place the author, as individual, on an altar.

For some *Upaniṣads,* not even the names of the authors are known. On the other hand, for one who has shed the sense of ego (*ahaṁkāra*), how could he express himself with the individuality of name and form?

With reference to the traditional teachings it is necessary to offer an additional consideration: when one speaks of *Brahmā, Brahman, ahaṁkāra*, or – as the pre-Socratics expressed themselves – of Eros, Being, fire, air, water etc., this is because the empirical formal mind can understand only if very precise names are given to those particularly abstract Principles, putting them also in time/space. *Brahman*, Being, etc., are impersonal Principles, are 'states of awareness', 'states of being' that have neither name nor form. When one talks about Love, Knowledge, etc., the dianoetic mind needs to 'materialize' them in a specific form; as an example, the Love of which Christianity speaks, although 'a state of being' needs to be given a well-defined form which is Jesus. But 'God is adored in spirit and truth.'

However, it can be said that Jesus, through that human form, 'incarnates' the Principle of Love. Likewise Plato, through that human form, incarnates the Principle of Knowledge/wisdom. Likewise it can be said regarding Śaṅkara, Gauḍapāda, etc., that they incarnate Knowledge/wisdom.

Up to this point, this condition can be considered normal. The problem arises when the mind, unable to grasp the Principle, which is behind the form, *identifies* it with the name, thus arousing struggles, even with weapons, in order for the name belonging to that specific ecclesiastical community to predominate.

The *Upaniṣads* talk about the Sun. Plato has those who had fallen into generation come out of the 'Cave' and brings them back to the splendor of the Sun. Akhenaton of ancient Egypt made a revolution when he proposed worshiping the Sun. The Sun, although the same for everybody and something that no one can appropriate, is the visible symbol of an 'invisible' Reality, which needs to be perceived through intuition.

Hence the 'Lesser Mysteries' are for the majority of humanity, while the 'Greater Mysteries' are for those persons able to comprehend the Symbol as well as what is behind the Symbol. Orphism contemplates both the Lesser Mysteries and the Greater Mysteries, it can therefore be said of it that it is a complete Teaching.[1]

Pythagoras, Parmenides, Plato, Plotinus, etc. and all of those who succeeded them, availed themselves of the Greater Mysteries.

Without the Greater Mysteries we would not have authentic Metaphysics in its true essence. Considering this, we can quote a truly emblematic passage by Plato:

---

[1] Cf. *Orphism and the Initiatory Tradition*, by Raphael. Aurea Vidyā, New York.

'And they were certainly not fools, those who instituted the Mysteries: and truly already from ancient times they have revealed to us in a veiled way that one who arrives to Hades without being initiated and without having purified himself, will lie in the mire; on the other hand, one who has been initiated and has purified himself, arriving there, will live with the gods. In fact, the interpreters of the Mysteries say that 'the bearers of ferulles are many, but the Bacchuses are few.' And these, I believe, are none other than those who practice philosophy correctly.'[1]

R.

[1] Plato, *Phaedo* 69c-d.

*1. The mind is stated to be: pure and impure. The impure mind is determined by desires, the pure mind is devoid of desire.*

What is called mind is divided into *buddhi* and *manas*. Both have the faculty of knowing; but while the *buddhi* is of an intuitive, noetic order, the mind or *manas* is a type of inferior mind which utilizes the five senses, which are not perfect either, in order to know things; it corresponds to the *diánoia* of Plato, while the first is a faculty of the *noûs*.

Within the *manas* operates the *ahaṁkāra* (= that which forms the empirical ego), the sense of 'I', or ego, which refers everything to itself, thus the 'mine', the 'yours', etc., are born.

With the *ahaṁkāra* arises the separation among the various entities, and even worse, a split with the universal, with the intelligible, is created which determines the drama of the human being.

The whole can be synthesized in the following diagram:

*jīvātman*

↓

*jīva* ⟶ *buddhi*, *manas*, *ahaṁkāra* } Psychic aspect

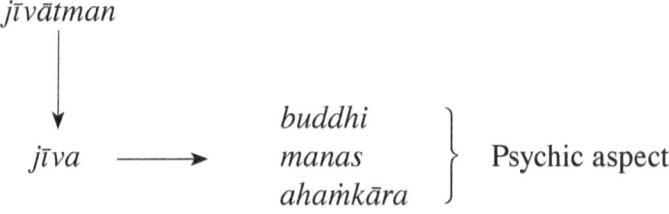

The first *yoga* movement, in order to be able to knowingly join the universal, or even better, to unveil the *jīva,* must be that of recognizing the polar distinction of the universal and the individual that live together in the human being. The being can therefore constitute the Whole or the part depending on how the 'spotlight' of the mind is directed. Therefore the problem is not the mind as such, but is the *ahaṁkāra* that needs to be resolved.[1]

2. *For the human being the mind is the cause of both bondage and liberation: when it is joined with objects [it leads] to bondage, when it is devoid of objects it is called liberation.*[2]

The mental substance is that which creates conflict or harmony, depending on the specific configuration it takes.

For the resolving of this type of mind here are some *sūtras* of the *Yogadarśana.*

> '*Yoga* is the suspension of the modifications of the mind (*cittavṛtti*).
>
> [When this has been effected] then the seer rests in its essential nature.
>
> In the other modalities [when the seer is not founded in himself] there is identification with the modifications [of the mind].'[3]

---

[1] To further clarify, see Raphael's commentaries to the following texts: *Vivekacūḍāmaṇi*, *Dṛgdṛśyaviveka*, and *Bhagavadgītā*. Aurea Vidyā, New York.

[2] See also, *Maitry Upaniṣad* VI.34.11.

[3] Patañjali, *The Regal Way to Realization* (*Yogadarśana*) I.2-4. Op.cit.

*3. Since the mind, uncoupled from the sensory objects, [is] favorable to liberation, it, thus devoid of the object, [represents] the goal of the constant aspiration to liberation.*

'The mental sheath represents the sacrificial fire and projects the whole of phenomenal world. This fire is fed by the numerous desires of the five senses, which are the priests, acting as a continuous stream of oblations.'

'Beyond the mind (*manas*) there is no more ignorance (*avidyā*). In fact, ignorance is the mind, the cause of rebirth. When this is dissolved, everything is dissolved; when it manifests, everything appears.'

'The wind gathers the clouds, and the same wind dispels them. In the same way the mind imagines bondage, but also imagines liberation.'[1]

*4. [It is necessary to] eliminate the attachment of the senses to the objects and fold the mind into the heart (*hṛd*); when the* ātmā *arrives at abandoning the thought modifications it attains the supreme state.*

We propound again our notes to *śloka* 174 of the *Vivekacūḍāmaṇi* because they are relevant to this *sūtra*:

'The mind, before obtaining the state of serenity, without desire for acquisition, generally passes through five states of adaptation:

[1] Śaṅkara, *Vivekacūḍāmaṇi* 168, 169, 172. Op. cit.

1. The mind is totally bewildered (*kṣipta*). In this condition *rajas* is powerful and conditioning. The mind is assailed by external stimuli.

2. The mind appears darkened and blind (*mūḍha*). In this condition *tamas* exercises its influence. It seems at times that a veil has come down over the mind, making it 'non-perceptive', absent, and obnubilated by *tamas*.

3. The mind is agitated (*vikṣipta*). The agitation may take place because of random emotions or because the mind's particular structure presents some imperfections.

4. The mind is recollected into a single point (*ekāgra*). This means that a certain control of the *vṛttis* or thought modifications, has been attained, but there remain subconscious tendencies in the latent state to be neutralized.

5. The mind is harmonious (*samāpati*). In this condition no subconscious tendencies nor any external stimuli penetrate into the consciousness without the assent of the inner thinker.

Thoughts are a continuum/discontinuum; in order to resolve and to understand the flow of the mental becoming and non-becoming, it is necessary to interject oneself into the interstices between two ideas and remain in that void/ transcendence, as long as possible.'[1]

*5. [The mind] must be fully reabsorbed into the heart until the cessation [of its activity], this is knowledge and meditation, the rest is erudite exposition.*

[1] Notes by Raphael to Śaṅkara's *Vivekacūḍāmaṇi* 174. Op. cit.

This *sūtra*, as the preceding ones, is very important because it explains the thinking process and the vital universal mechanism of the 'continuum/discontinuum.'

The mind remains silent not by way of simple inhibition or by forcing it to take certain positions; it becomes quiescent when the fuel has been removed from it. The desire is, thus, the energy of the *rajas* that pushes towards agitation, towards psychological restlessness and to the continuity of the phenomenal translational movement.

*Sūtras* 32 and 33 of Chapter IV of the *Yogasūtra* can be of great help to better understand this movement.

> 'Therefore, the [three] *guṇas* having achieved their purpose, the process [in them] of modifications reaches its end.'
>
> 'The change related to the moments (*kṣaṇa*), and which is knowable at the end [of the modification], is the succession (*krama*).'[1]

The cessation of the continuous modifications of the *prakṛti* (the primary base of any vital phenomenon) happens when the dissociation between *puruṣa* and *prakṛti*, which represent the two principial poles – positive and negative, active and passive – of any objective phenomenon, occurs. Thus, as an example at the gross physical level, the electrical current stops when, in a dynamo, the magnetic field has been removed. What leads to the union of two data, which in their turn gives birth to a vital process, is the stimulating, exciting, magnetic power. At a certain level of existence, the instinctual psychological

---

[1] Patañjali, *The Regal Way to Realization* (*Yogadarśana*) IV.32-33. Op. cit.

desire constitutes exactly the stimulating electromagnetic *fiat* capable of producing the phenomenon/event.

The Buddha, being interested in the nature of desire, discovered that desire is the primary incentive for the continuity of the human ego as appearance on the scene of the phenomenal life. The electrical desire pushes the mental substance into incessant modifications whose successions, which are related to the moments or to the rhythmical impulses, create the continuous formal existence, in other words, the becoming.

The succession, therefore, is constituted by the uninterrupted perpetuity of moments and is perceived in the final stage of every modification. The word *kṣaṇa* of *sūtra* 33 of Patañjali literally means 'instant.'

According to the conception of the *Upaniṣad*, time is not something that is always continuous, rather it is discontinuous. The modern scientific researches have demonstrated the validity of this theory because it has been discovered that the vital phenomena are not continuous, as was previously thought, but discontinuous, because matter is composed of separate corpuscles that are interrelated by empty... spaces. Therefore, light is nothing but the composition of photonic 'quanta', separated one from the other, and showing the character of discontinuity.

The *Upaniṣads* had already highlighted that the continuous series of changes that take place in the threefold phenomenal world, and which give us the measure of time, is not uninterrupted, even if our imperfect senses do not perceive the underlying reality. This same event occurs at the cinema: the movie, which seems apparently continuous, represents instead the product of a series of separate images projected in rapid succession on the screen.

'The universe, being an uninterrupted series of perceptions of *Brahmā*...'

'The mind, the cause of false notions, becomes perfectly calm for the Sage who has known *Brahman*...'[1]

Therefore, every modification that occurs in the world of the phenomenal *prakṛti* produces a consequent sensory impression in our consciousness/mind, which, due to its speed, makes such modifications appear as continuous, when it is instead discontinuous. The instance of the frame/phenomenon is called *kṣaṇa* and the entire process, which after all represents the becoming of things, is called *krama*.

All this is synthetically contained in *sūtra* 33 of Patañjali and constitutes the esoteric base of the first *sūtra* of the present *Upaniṣad*. It is well to consider that every spiritual work should be framed in the philosophical and metaphysical context of the entire traditional Doctrine.

Now, the consciousness of the seeker, as long as it is implicated in the process, will not be able to understand its real nature and that of the things/events. To be able to grasp the sense of the authentic life, the *yogi* must know how to leave the sequence of *māyā* and put himself beyond the movement/becoming/appearance, in order to not be bounced from one frame/phenomenon to the next. Between one idea and the next a hiatus exists, a void, which has to be conquered, dilated and stabilized; this implies being able to slow down the discontinuous succession of thought/desire and being able to leave the mental process/becoming.

---

[1] Śaṅkara, *Vivekacūḍāmaṇi* 521.526. Op. cit.

Beyond the phenomenon/appearance, a substratum which constitutes the Unconditioned or the Non-Being exists, i.e. that screen on which the phenomena are silhouetted in a discontinuous mode. To grasp the Non-Being (Absolute), leaving the power of the attractive and gravitational *māyā*, means to put oneself beyond the manifest, which means to '... bring the mind back into the heart, until one has arrived at [its] solution: this is knowledge, this is liberation. The rest is nothing but bookish verbosity.'[1]

*6. It is not conceivable nor is it inconceivable, it is conceivable and [at the same time] inconceivable; [comprehending thus] one realizes* Brahman *without parts.*

Depending on the position of consciousness in which one places oneself, *Brahman* can be seen as conceivable or inconceivable, or as one and the other together.

*7. Yoga, in order to [realize] the supreme state, avails itself of the completely indistinct sound. With the indistinct [sound] one favors the state of Being, and not that of the non-being.*

The sacred syllable *Om* represents the symbol of *Brahmā*. By bringing the *Om* into its indistinctiveness one arrives at the supreme state of *nirguṇa*.

> 'In truth, he becomes one who fulfills desires, he who, knowing this [syllable] thus, meditates on the syllable [*Om*] as the *Udgītha*.'[2]

---

[1] *Maitry Upaniṣad* VI.34.8.

[2] *Chāndogya Upaniṣad* I.I.7.

The syllable composed of the three *mātras* (A U M; the first two vowels contract into O) possesses, in truth, four elements; the fourth though, represented by the entire sound in its principial aspect, is not expressed by a particular *mātra* because it pre-exists any distinction or modification. In other words, it is sensorily inaudible and in-articulable. Because of this, the *sūtra* in question invites one to gradually enter into the without sound (*amātra*) and unveil the identity with the Being/ *Brahman* in that pure and sole supreme Being.[1]

The *Māṇḍūkya Upaniṣad* demonstrates the correspondence of the sacred monosyllable *Om* and of its constituent elements (*mātras*) with *Brahman/ātman* and its four parts (*pādas*), in addition to the effects of the meditation on *Om*.

For better comprehension we refer to the first *sūtras* of the *Māṇḍūkya Upaniṣad* (I-VII) which treat of this theme:

'I. *Om! Om* is all this. A clear explanation follows: that which is past, present and future is truly *Om*. And that which is beyond this threefold temporality, in truth, is always *Om*.

Śaṅkara comments: 'As all the objects which are signified with names do not differ from those names, and also, as the names do not differ in any way from *Om*, likewise all that which is cannot but be *Om*. In the same manner as one thing is known with the name which is appropriate to it, likewise

---

[1] *Brahman*, as it is inconceivable and inexpressible, is generally designated by negation, because no qualification or attribute can be given to It. Therefore, *Brahman* is the pure and unwavering One-without-a-second. *Īśvara* is designated as the Being in that it represents the *Personification* of a Principle, it is the ontological state. The simple non-being, instead, constitutes all that which is the world of the sensible, therefore the becoming/process: this so as to avoid confusions of terms.

the supreme *Brahman* cannot be known but by its name: *Om*. This supreme *Brahman* is, really, *Om*...

And if the *sūtra* talks about a clear explanation, it is because *Om* constitutes the means by which to attain *Brahman*, in addition to being its most adherent expression.

All that which is conditioned by the threefold temporality: past, present and future, represents equally *Om* for the reasons already expounded.

All that which is beyond this threefold temporality and which can be inferred by its effects, but which is not circumscribed by time, is called the non manifest: and also this, in truth, is *Om*.'[1]

II. All this is verily *Brahman*. This *ātman* is *Brahman* and the *ātman* has four quarters (*pādas*).

III. The first quarter is *vaiśvānara*, whose sphere [of action] is the waking state; it is conscious of external objects, it has seven limbs and nineteen mouths; it experiences gross (material) objects.

IV. The second quarter is *taijasa* (the luminous), whose sphere of action is the dream state; consciousness here is interiorized. It has seven limbs and nineteen mouths and experiences subtle objects.

V. This is the state of deep sleep in which the sleeper no longer enjoys any object nor experiences any dream. The third quarter is *prājña* whose sphere of activity is, in fact, deep sleep; here all things remain undifferentiated; in truth, it is a unity of pure consciousness. (In *prājña*) there is fullness of happiness

---

[1] Commentary by Śaṅkara to *sūtra* I of the *Māṇḍūkya Upaniṣad* with the *kārikās* of Guaḍapāda.

and (the sleeper) truly tests this happiness. It is the cognitive condition (of the other two states).

VI. It (*prājña*) is the supreme Lord, the Omniscient, the inner Ruler, the Source of all; in it all things originate and dissolve.

VII. The Sages believe that the Fourth – which has knowledge neither of the internal (*tijasa*) world nor of the external (*viśva*) world, nor simultaneously of the former and the latter, and which, ultimately, is not (even) a unity of integral consciousness, as it is neither conscious nor unconscious – is *adṛṣṭa*: invisible, *avyavahārya*: non-agent, *agrāhya*: incomprehensible, *alakṣana*: indefinable, *acintya*: unthinkable, *avyapadeśya*: indescribable; it is the only *pratyayasāra*: essence of self-knowledge, without any trace of manifestation, fullness of peace and bliss devoid of duality: it is the *ātman* and as such it must be known.'[1]

In reference to the Fourth, or *Brahman nirguṇa*, Śaṅkara, in his commentary to the *Bṛhadāraṇyaka Upaniṣad*, writes: '[*Nirguṇa*] *Brahman* can be [indirectly] indicated only through name, form and the activity which are superimposed on it, by means of expressions such as the following ones and others: '*Brahman* is knowledge and bliss' (*Bṛ.* 3.9.28) '... it is truly constituted in one absolute unity of pure consciousness.' (*Bṛ.* 2.4.12), or [directly] by means of terms such as *Brahman* or *ātman* (*Bṛ.* 2.3.6). If instead we wanted to describe precisely its authentic nature, which transcends all the qualifications determined by the superimpositions, then it cannot be indicated

[1] Gauḍapāda, *Māṇḍūkyakārikā*, *Āgama Prakaraṇa*, *sūtras* I-VII of the *Upaniṣad*, by Raphael. Op. cit.

in any way. In this instance there is just this method, i.e. the designations in the terms: 'not this, not this' (*neti neti*; *neti* = *na* + *iti*), through which are progressively eliminated all the qualifications that might be attributed to it.'[1]

*Vaiśvānara* is represented by the first *mātra* A. *Taijasa*, by the second *mātra* U. *Prājña*, by the third *mātra* M because it is the measure of the other two *mātras* and also because it is the ultimate goal as it contains the synthesis of all the sounds.

These *mātras* have their geometrical correspondences: point, line and volume. The point is the principial state of all of the geometrical figures, as, on the other hand, *prājña* is the principle of all the states of manifestation, the unity without dimension.

The effects that are obtained with meditation on the sound *Om* correspond to certain degrees of realization that can be expressed as follows: the first *mātra* constitutes the full development of the corporeal individuality; the second, the actualization of the integral extension of the individuality as such, in its extra-corporeal possibilities; the third, the realization of the supra-individual states; the fourth, the identity with the supreme *Brahman*.

In the commentary to the first *sūtra* of the *Dṛgdṛśyaviveka* one can read:

> 'All forms are simply clusters of energy living in time and space which manifest certain distinct qualities.'

It is this sound that the present *Upaniṣad* invites us to recognize. As it was already mentioned, both in the Vedic Orient and in the West, the philosophical conception of sound as constructive element of the universe was already known.

---

[1] *Bṛhadāraṇyaka Upaniṣad* with the commentary of Śaṅkara, II.III.6.

Saint John states: 'In the beginning was the Word [sound] ... All things were made by Him; and without Him was not any thing made that was made.'

The *Qabbālāh* teaches that sound, light and number are the three main factors of creation. The Pythagoreans maintained that the world was evoked from 'Chàos' (the quiet Darkness or *prakṛti* at the pre-genetic, pre-formal state, or at the undifferentiated state; 'Darkness' since the *Fiat lux* has not yet darted) through sound or Harmony and made in accordance with the principles of the musical ratios. Now, a musical note is highlighted by the interval; or rather, it is the interval itself that reveals the note giving it life and value; it is the interval that represents the silent, unexpressed substratum, but which is fundamental and essential.

It is, therefore, necessary to bring the sound *Om*, as it is suggested by the present *sūtra*, up to the highest consciential frequency, so that it will not be perceivable any longer, and to put the noumenal awareness (*cit*) within 'the unexpressed and silent interval', it is there where the Being can be attained.

In order to realize what has just been expounded it is necessary, before anything else, to have the initial qualification, which is: the request on the part of the consciousness for the awakening of other existential possibilities. This is why certain teachings cannot be received by all people because, for them, the time has not yet come. But, for sure, sooner or later the time will come because there in all beings is the *jīva*, there is the *ātman*, and this serves the purpose of realizing the Awakening.

*8. This [Being] is in fact* Brahman *undivided, exempt from differentiation, without blemish. This* Brahman *is my very self. Realizing this knowledge one is* Brahman *itself, this is certain.*

The screen on which the rhythmical harmonics of sound are woven, the existential continuum/discontinuum, is *Brahman*, the One-without-a-second, which cannot be subdivided into parts, possesses no distinctions, produces neither action/movement/change nor modifications.

> 'Thirty rays converge into the hub
> But the use of the carriage is in the void of the hub.
> The vases are made of clay
> But the use of the vase is in its void.
> Walls, doors and windows make a house
> But the use of the house is in its void
> Therefore from being [as becoming] comes possession
> [Therefore conflict.]
> In the Non-Being [in the Void, as true Fullness]
> Is the essence.'[1]

*9. Without distinction, without end, inaccessible to rational discursiveness, non-measurable, without origin; in this way the knower of knowledge makes himself free.*

> 'Realize that *Brahman* whose splendor illumines the sun and the other stars, but which is not illumined by their light, [that *Brahman*] thanks to whom all this [universe] is manifested.'[2]

> 'To one to whom it is unknown, it is, on the other hand, known. To someone to whom it [is] known, it is, on the other hand, unknown. It is unknown to those who [believe

---

[1] Lao-Tze, *Tao-Tê-Ching* 11.

[2] Śaṅkara, *ātmabodha* 61. Aurea Vidyā, New York.

that they] know it, while it is known by those who [believe] that they do not know it.'[1]

*10. There is neither death nor birth nor a* sādhaka *who is in bondage nor [anybody] who desires liberation nor is there liberation. This is the supreme truth.*[2]

> 'There is thus neither birth nor death, no one who is imprisoned and no one struggling; there is no liberation and no disciple seeking liberation: this is the supreme truth (*paramārthatā*).'
>
> 'Bondage and liberation, created by the play of *māyā*, do not exist in reality within the *ātman*, just as the illusory snake, which appears and disappears, does not exist in the rope, whose nature undergoes no change.'[3]

*11. There is only one* ātmā *in the states of waking, dreaming and deep sleep. One who will be able to go beyond the three states will no longer know [the concept of] rebirth [and therefore of death.]*

One is therefore in front of three states of consciousness at the different frequencies that the *jīva* expresses and experiences. But can one state, as much as it differs in vibratory tone, be maintained as superior or inferior to another? What makes one believe that the gross solid state, the one normally

---

[1] *Kena Upaniṣad* II.3.

[2] See also, *Māṇḍūkyakārikā* II.32, by Raphael. Op. cit.

[3] Śaṅkara, *Vivekacūḍāmaṇi*, *ślokas* 574 and 569. See also the relevant commentary by Raphael. Op. cit.

observed with the usual sensory instruments of relation, should be superior and more real than the other two?

In the Notes to the *Sarvasāra Upaniṣad* there have been given indications which are sufficient to make one reflect on certain implications that can emerge when one wants to investigate into such existential states. See in particular Note 4 on page 69.

*12. The one* ātman *dwells in every being, just as the moon is reflected in [multiple surfaces] of water. It is seen as One or as multiple [depending on the position of consciousness].*

*13. Just as a jar can be destroyed, but not the space enclosed within it, likewise is for the [body of the]* jīva, *which is of the same nature as the jar.*

> 'Before its appearance it could not exist, and after its disappearance it will never be able to exist. Its parabola is just a flash. Its qualities are impermanent.
> It is by nature subject to change. It is composed of parts, inert, and like a jug, it is a mere sensory object. Can such a body ever possibly be the *ātman*, the indestructible Witness of all phenomenal changes?'[1]

What is that which, without an antecedent or subsequent, appears to our eyes? That body/individual, not having a before nor an after, what can it represent? What value can be given to that which is wont to appear and disappear? That which never was nor will ever be, can it ever be? A datum is real

[1] Śaṅkara, *Vivekacūḍāmaṇi* 155. Op. cit.

because it was, is, and will always be; but that which was not and will not be, how can it be?

*14. Its different forms shatter continuously like a jar and, nonetheless [the* jīva*] lives eternally.*

'That which is other than this is perishable.'[1]

*15. If one is clouded by the* māyā *of sound/word, is not dwelling in the lotus of the heart; once the clouding is eliminated, the unity (*eka*) is recognized.*

*16. The sound/word which is not destroyed when it has ceased to resound, is the supreme* Brahman*; the knower should meditate on that which has not perished in order to [realize] the peace of the* ātman.

*17. Two sciences must be known: that of the* Brahman *of the sound/word, and that of the supreme* Brahman. *One who knows well the* Brahman *of the sound/word also attains the supreme* Brahman.

The word can be considered as the Word or the first sound containing the universal life. The principial sound constitutes the *saguṇa Brahman* or qualified *Īśvara*, the God-person, the first cause of all which is. All of this can find its raison d'être because there is a foundation, the *nirguṇa Brahman*, that gives it the possibility of being what it is. Every form, to whatever

---

[1] *Bṛhadāraṇyaka Upaniṣad* III.IV.2.

dimension it might belong, is the result of a sound which, at lower levels, manifests as light.

To know the intimate numerical and geometric combination, means to know the primordial archetype that dwells in *Īśvara*.

We thus have two sciences: that which leads to *saguṇa Brahman*, as informal primordial sound, and that which leads to *nirguṇa Brahman*, upon which the former depends. But the science of the *saguṇa* sound cannot but gradually lead to the sound without movement, or to the very essence of Sound.

The further that a being is from the Point (*amṛtabindu* = Principial point without dimension), the greater are its sonorous agitations and its volume. The actualization of inner states leads to 're-entering the heart', conceived as the great Silence or profound Peace. The Islamic Tradition (and it is necessary to remember that there is a single Tradition with different 'adaptations' in time and space) states that there are three types of *dhikr*: that of the lips, that of the mind, and that of the heart. They are three stages of 're-entry' or retirement that is more and more interiorized, then transcendent, then taking the Word back to its own metaphysical source.

*18. The knower, after having meditated upon them, abandons the treatises about the lower knowledge, just as someone who, searching for the seed, abandons the bark.*

*19. The cows have different colors, while milk has just one color. Knowledge must be considered as the milk and one who is anchored to distinctions as the cows.*

*20. As the butter is concealed in the milk, likewise intelligence dwells in every being. It has to be manifested through the intellect as support.*

*21. With knowledge as a cane, one has to bring fire to its extinction. One should meditate: 'Undivided, immobile, and pacified, this* Brahman *is myself.'*

*22. All beings dwell in Him, and He in all the beings. I am That, Vāsudeva! I am That, Vāsudeva!*

The Point (*bindu*), without dimension, without form, time and space, is *Brahman*, and this *Brahman* is the essence of all the beings. The *Vedānta* concludes that only *Brahman* exists and that the *jīvātman* is nothing but a ray, a spark of the *Brahman*,[1] therefore this *mantra* must be realized: '*Ahaṁ brahmāsmi*: I *[jīva]* am *Brahman*' (*Bṛhadāranyaka Upaniṣad* I.IV.10).

*Here ends the Amṛtabindu Upaniṣad*

[1] Cf. *Muṇḍaka Upaniṣad* II.1.2.

# *Atharvaśira Upaniṣad*

## INTRODUCTION

The *Śira Upaniṣad*, 'Head', 'Apex' or principal *Upaniṣad* of the *Atharva Veda,* is considered to be of a monistic tendency and more precisely Shaiva. Here *Śiva* takes the aspect of Rudra as the principial Unity.

In the first part there is a dialogue between the Gods and Rudra himself. In other words, the disciples ask the god Rudra for the teaching, and he responds.

Rudra, through his power of deployment (*śakti*), represents the entire cosmos.

Having received the teaching, the Gods pay Rudra homage with a series of statements of a rhythmical and harmonic order (this is evident in the Sanskrit text).

To someone who is unfamiliar with the initiatory process of the *Upaniṣads* certain expressions and repetitions could seem absurd, but not to those who comprehend the subtle function of sound/rhythm.

The *Upaniṣads* are not theoretical speculations in themselves, but represent the modalities of traditional order that are expounded to the disciples to awaken their consciousness to the supreme Truth.

Let us, for instance, consider the following statements of the text:

Rudra is the Blissful, he is also the Great: homage, homage be rendered to Him.

Rudra is the Blissful, he is also the earth: homage, homage be rendered to Him.

Rudra is the Blissful, he is also the intermediate region: homage, homage be rendered to Him.

Rudra is the Blissful, he is also the sky: homage, homage be rendered to Him.

Here, the following are highlighted:

1. An evocatory rhythm with a consequent,
2. Awakening of a specific higher center (*cakra*);
3. An abstraction from the sensory thinking process and a hold of the synthetic intuition;
4. A meditation with seed.

Rudra is the Blissful. Here the accent is put on *ānanda* (bliss), an expression consubstantial with Rudra. The One is pure Bliss; one who attains the One, or rather, is re-integrated into the principial One, will be *ānanda*, Joy without desire. The *Upaniṣad* therefore invites us to unveil this joy without an object.

The meditation focuses on certain aspects of Rudra: the Great, as *Mahat*, cosmic essence/substance without form, the root from which everything draws its origin: the earth as the gross sphere; the intermediate region as the subtle sphere[1] (see the fourth *pāda* of this *Upaniṣad*: 'Why is it called subtle? Because as soon as it is pronounced, becoming subtle, it masters

[1] The subtle world is made up of different types of *prāṇa* and is the substratum of the gross sphere, which it vitalizes. The stabilization of these subtle energies determines a corresponding and automatic mastery of the gross physical plane.

the bodies and seizes the limbs; because of this, it is called subtle.') and the sky as the causal/germinal sphere. But all this process/becoming is subjected to the Principial Being.

The meditation, conducted with intelligence, on the objective/sensible levels first, and then on the intuitive/synthetic ones, unveils the knowledge, and therefore the realization of the corresponding states of consciousness.

The fourth part or *pāda* is an application of the *praṇava Om* dealt with in the third section. The *oṁkāra*, the sacred syllable *Om*, is *Śiva* himself, or Rudra.

In the fifth *pāda* there is a description, almost tantric, of the meditation on the separate syllables of the *oṁkāra* corresponding to the three aspect of Rudra (*Brahmā, Viṣṇu* and *Śiva*) and towards the end the emphasis is placed on the Shaiva vision of the *pāśupatas*.

In the sixth *pāda* the meditation focuses on Rudra as creator, conservator, and transformer of the worlds. It also constitutes a cosmogonic synthesis of a certain interest.

In the seventh *pāda* the fruits that are obtained by realizing the content of the *Upaniṣad* are enumerated.

R.

## I

*Om*. The Gods, having gone to the celestial worlds, asked Rudra: 'Who are you?'

Rudra replied: 'In the origin I was alone, still now I am alone, and I will always be alone, there is nothing outside of me.[1*] I am imbued with interiority and I dwell in the depths of the worlds (regions). I am permanent and impermanent, manifested and not manifested.[2] I am *Brahmā* and not *Brahmā*. I am the East and the West. I am the South and the North. I am the nadir and the zenith. I am all the regions. I am the masculine, the feminine, and the neutral principles. I am the sacred *mantra* (*gāyatrī*). I am the hymn that is sung to the sun. I am the meter of eleven syllables, that of twelve syllables, and that of eight syllables. I am the sacred text (*chando*). I am the household fire. I am the fire of the South, and the fire of the oblations. I am the truth (*satyo 'ham*). I am the cow. I am Gauri. I am the *Ṛg Veda*, I am the *Yajur Veda*. I am the *Sāma Veda*, I am the *Arthava Veda* of the *Aṅgiras*. I am the first-born. I am the best. I am the most extended. I am the waters. I am the fire. I am the concealed. I am the hermit of the forest. I am the eternal and also the transient. I am the blue lotus. I am the purifier. I am the powerful. I am the inner, the

---

* The reference numbers are to the Notes at the end of the *Upaniṣad*, starting on page 124..

median, and the outer. I am the primeval light. Such I am, in truth, and all must know me in this way. The one who knows me, knows all the Gods, all the *Vedas* and all the Scriptures that are connected to them. He is *Brahman* for the *brāhmaṇa*, the cow for the bulls, the *brāhmaṇa* for the sacerdotal character, the oblation for the clarified butter, the vital power for the nourishment, the truth for the true, the virtue (*dharma*) for the sacred: I satisfy them with my own ardor.'

Then the Gods interrogated Rudra, they went towards Rudra, they meditated on Him, and, with arms raised, they glorified Rudra:

## II

1. *Om.* Rudra is the Blissful, he is also *Brahmā*, homage, homage be rendered to Him.

2. Rudra is the Blissful, he is also *Viṣṇu*, homage, homage be rendered to Him.

3. Rudra is the Blissful, he is also Skanda, homage, homage be rendered to Him.

4. Rudra is the Blissful, he is also Indra, homage, homage be rendered to Him.

5. Rudra is the Blissful, he is also Agni, homage, homage be rendered to Him.

6. Rudra is the Blissful, he is also Vāyu, homage, homage be rendered to Him.

7. Rudra is the Blissful, he is also Sūrya, homage, homage be rendered to Him.

8. Rudra is the Blissful, he is also Soma, homage, homage be rendered to Him.

9. Rudra is the Blissful, he contains the eight planets: homage, homage be rendered to Him.

10. Rudra is the Blissful, he also represents the eight planets of inverse movement: homage, homage be rendered to Him.

11. Rudra is the Blissful, he is also the mystical word *Bhūḥ*: homage, homage be rendered to Him.

12. Rudra is the Blissful, he is also the mystical word *Bhuvaḥ*: homage, homage be rendered to Him.

13. Rudra is the Blissful, he is also the mystical word *Svaḥ*: homage, homage be rendered to Him.

14. Rudra is the Blissful, he is also the Great: homage, homage be rendered to Him.

15. Rudra is the Blissful, he is also the earth: homage, homage be rendered to Him.

16. Rudra is the Blissful, he is also the intermediate region: homage, homage be rendered to Him.

17. Rudra is the Blissful, he is also the sky: homage, homage be rendered to Him.

18. Rudra is the Blissful, he is also the waters: homage, homage be rendered to Him.

19. Rudra is the Blissful, he is also the resplendent [material] fire: homage, homage be rendered to Him.

20. Rudra is the Blissful, he is also time: homage, homage be rendered to Him.

21. Rudra is the Blissful, he is also the God of death (Yama): homage, homage be rendered to Him.

22. Rudra is the Blissful, he is also death: homage, homage be rendered to Him.

23. Rudra is the Blissful, he is also immortality: homage, homage be rendered to Him.

24. Rudra is the Blissful, he is also space: homage, homage be rendered to Him.

25. Rudra is the Blissful, he is also the universe: homage, homage be rendered to Him.

26. Rudra is the Blissful, he is also that which is gross: homage, homage be rendered to Him.

27. Rudra is the Blissful, he is also that which is subtle: homage, homage be rendered to Him.

28. Rudra is the Blissful, he is also that which is resplendent: homage, homage be rendered to Him.

29. Rudra is the Blissful, he is also that which is obscurity: homage, homage be rendered to Him.

30. Rudra is the Blissful, he is also the totality: homage, homage be rendered to Him.

31. Rudra is the Blissful, he is also the Real: homage, homage be rendered to Him.

32. Rudra is the Blissful, he is also the indivisible universal totality: homage, homage be rendered to Him.

## III

*Bhūḥ* is your origin, *bhuvaḥ* is your intermediate space, *svaḥ* is your head.[3] He who unveils all the forms, the one *Brahmā* is you; you are dual, trine, you are the expanse, the peace, the abundance; you are the oblation and that which is not an object of sacrifice, you are the donation, and that which cannot be donated, the all and the part, the universal and the particular, you are the effect and the cause, you are the supreme and the not supreme, you are the absolute. We have drunk the *soma*[4] and we have discovered ourselves to be immortal, we have penetrated the light and found the Gods. Then how could any offense harm us?

How, O Immortal, can the deceit of the mortal reach us?

The subtle *puruṣa* was before the Sun and the Moon.[5]

But is not the whole universe contained in Him? The *puruṣa,* due to its own ardor, incorporates that which has the nature of Prajāpati,[6] that which is subtle, that which has the nature of the *soma*; the comprehensible as far as that which is comprehensible; the being for its being; the nature of the *soma* for the nature of the *soma*, the subtle for the fact of being subtle, the aeriform for that which is ethereal: homage, homage be rendered to Him, the Transformer, the great Omni-pervasive.

All the divinities are held in the heart; all the *prāṇas* are established in the heart; in the heart you are eternally He who masters the three elements of the *oṁkāra*.

Its head is situated in the North and its feet the South. That which is situated in the North is the *oṁkāra*; the *oṁkāra* is the *praṇava*,[7] the *praṇava* is omnipresent; the omnipresent is infinite; the infinite is the savior; the savior is subtle; the subtle is pure; that which is pure has the nature of the splendor; that which has the nature of the splendor is the pre-eminent (*para*) *Brahmā*; the pre-eminent *Brahmā* is the One; that which is the One is Rudra, that which is Rudra is the Lord, and the Lord is the blessed, the great Lord (*maheśvara*).

## IV

Now, why is it called *oṁkāra*? Because, as soon as it is pronounced it exhales the *prāṇa*: this is why it is called *oṁkāra*.

Why is it called *praṇava*? Because as soon as it is pronounced it takes the *brāhmaṇas* towards the *Brahman*; it is composed of the *Ṛg Veda*, the *Yajur Veda*, the *Sāma Veda*, the *Atharva Veda* of the *Aṅgiras*: this is why it is called *praṇava*.

Why is it called omnipresent? Because as soon as it is pronounced, It permeates every place like the fluid fat (*sneho*) pervades the sesame seed; under an invisible aspect it permeates the thread in all directions; this is why it is called omnipresent.

Why is it called infinite? Because, when it is pronounced, its limit cannot be discovered neither in terms of width, nor height nor depth: this is why it is called infinite.

Why is it called the savior? Because, as soon as it is pronounced it liberates from the great fear of birth, sickness, old-age, death and rebirth. [In doing so] It saves: this is why it is called the savior.

Why is it called pure? Because, as soon as it is pronounced, It calls back and purifies: this is why it is called pure (*śukla*).

Why is it called subtle? Because, as soon as it is pronounced, as it becomes subtle, it masters the bodies and seizes the limbs: this is why it is called subtle.

Why is it called 'The one that has the resplendent nature?' Because, as soon as it is pronounced, it renders [all things] luminous in the great obscurity: this is why it is called 'That one that has the resplendent nature.'

Why is it called pre-eminent *Brahmā*? Because it has the supreme perfection and represents the supreme goal. Mighty! Its mightiness is the cause of mightiness: this is why it is called pre-eminent *Brahmā*.

Why is it called sole? Because, having resolved all the *prāṇas* by consuming them, it is eternal. He reunites [the *prāṇas*] and disperses them; so that some return to their own source, while others go towards the south, the east, the north and the west. It reunites them all here and, united with them, it becomes sole, reabsorbing all beings: this is why it is called sole?[8]

Why is it called Rudra? Because only the *Ṛṣis* (seers) and none else can perceive its quality: this is why it is called Rudra.

Why is it called Lord, he who governs all the Gods through its creative and sovereign powers?

'To you, O Hero (*śūra*), we render praise, just as cows which have not yet been milked. Lord of the world, Lord that knows the sky, O Indra of the Lords, Immutable.'[9]

This is why it is called Lord.

Why is it called Blissful and great Lord? Because it grants knowledge to its followers and rewards them; it creates the word and emits it. The knowledge of the *ātman* and the power of *Yoga* exalt it and magnify it: this is why it is called the Blissful and the great Lord (*maheśvara*).

This is the work of Rudra.

## V

This divine being is one in all the regions of the universe and at the beginning he self-limited himself into a matrix. He resides within every being and is, therefore, present in all.[10] Sole Rudra, without a second, with his sovereign powers he is Lord of all the worlds.

In the hour of the abstraction He contracts himself and withdraws the universe back into himself: He is the protector of the worlds.[11]

He is Unity and lives in every matrix; through Him the world of names and forms totally unfolds itself. When one is able to discern this Lord, this *puruṣa*, this divine desirable being, one finally reaches profound peace (*śānti*).[12]

When [the beings] will leave this earth, the cause of bondage, and through the Intelligence will remit to Rudra what has been accumulated, they will call Rudra the Sole (*eka*), the ancient, the powerful whose energy confers the peace of death.[13]

Therefore when this Lord of the four syllables minus one half (*Aum*) penetrates into the soul, it spreads peace and liberates the creatures from bondage.

The first syllable [A] has *Brahmā* as its divinity, its color is red. Whoever meditates on it without relenting goes to the kingdom of *Brahmā*.[14]

The second syllable [U] has *Viṣṇu* as its divinity, its color is black. Whoever meditates on it without relenting attains the kingdom of *Viṣṇu*.

The third syllable [M] has *Īśa* as its divinity, its color is brown. Whoever meditates on it without relenting attains the kingdom of *Īśa*.[15]

The fourth semi-syllable has all the Gods as its divinity.

Having become silent and pure, it traverses the firmament, its color is the glow of crystal. Whoever meditates on it without relenting conquers the dwelling place of Bliss.

Because of this, one must render homage to it: the seer/Sages praise it without words because it is inaccessible.[16]

This is the path towards the north which the Gods, the Fathers, the seer/Sages go to, where every perfection is surpassed: this is the supreme goal.

It has as its measure the tip of a hair, it occupies the center of the heart, as omnipresent God, made of gold.[17]

Those who, with acute intelligence, dwelling in the *ātmā*, contemplate it, they know the Peace, and no one else.

Having placed in Him anger, impatience, thirst for existence (*tṛṣṇā*), the earth as origin of the causal chain, and having established with intelligence in Rudra all that has been accumulated, they will call Rudra the One (*eka*).

Because Rudra, due to its eternity, to its primordial force, to its creative power and to its ardor of ascent, is the ruler; that which is called fire (*agni*) is ashes, wind (*vāyu*) is ashes, water is ashes, and the terrestrial sun is ashes, the sky is ashes, so all is ashes; ashes are the intellect and its eyes; Paśupati made a vow to cover his limbs with ashes: this in fact is its ritual symbol. [Comprehending all this] the creatures can find liberation.[18]

## VI

This Rudra who is to be found in fire, in waters; this Rudra who penetrates the plants, this Rudra who has shaped all the worlds; homage, homage be rendered to Him.

This Rudra in the waters, this Rudra in the plants, this Rudra in the trees; Rudra who sustains the universe in activity and, being its sustainer, transforms the earth in double and triple form, as the serpents in the intermediate space: homage, homage be rendered to Him.

*Atharvan* has united head and heart and, having dominion of his forehead, stimulates from the top of the head; this is the summit of the *Atharvan*, made up of splendor; therefore the *prāṇa* and the mind keep watch over Him. The heavens are not protected by the divinities nor is the intermediate space nor these worlds; the whole universe is woven and interlaced only in Him, this is why no one else exists except Him. Nothing can surpass him, nor can anyone precede him. There is nothing that he has to accomplish.

With a thousand feet and one head, He penetrates this world and makes it go around.

Time has its origin in the Eternal, therefore it is said to be inherent in This. In truth, it is [always] the Blissful Rudra while he unfolds his years. When it rests, it gathers all creatures in itself; when it breathes, the darkness is ripped open; from darkness the waters are born. With one finger he agitates the waters; what is agitated in the cold becomes cold, producing foam; this one produces an egg, from the egg *Brahmā* is born, from *Brahmā* the wind is born, from it the sacred syllable (*oṁkāra*), from the sacred syllable the hymn to the sun (*sāvitrī*), from it the sacred word; from the sacred word (*gāyatrī*) the worlds have their origin; may the ascent and the truth be lauded so that they may spread the inebriating milk.

This is the supreme ascent, it is the waters, the light, the lymph, the immortal *Brahma*. *Bhūḥ, bhuvaḥ, svaḥ!* Thus, homage [to Him].

## VII

If the *brāhmaṇa*, not possessing the sacred science, meditates on this 'Head' of the *Atharva* (*atharvaśira*), he will possess it. If his conduct is objectionable, he will be able to make it laudable. Agni will purify him, Vāyu will purify him, Sūrya will purify him, Soma will purify him, the Truth will purify him; all the Gods will know him. He will have meditated upon all the *Vedas*; he will have dived in all the pure waters; he will have the merit of all the sacrifices; he will have uttered sixty-thousand *gāyatrīs*, uttered the epic Poems, the *Purāṇas*, the praises to Rudra one-hundred thousand times; he will have uttered the *praṇava* many times.

His gaze, spreading into the distance, will be able to purify the human generations up to the seventh. So says the Blissful, 'Head' of the *Atharva*; uttering it in full [the *brāhmaṇa*] becomes virtuous and purified of all actions.

Uttering it a second time he reaches the supreme Master of the *Gaṇas*. Uttering it a third time he enters the Reality which is the sacred syllable *Om*. *Om!* Reality. *Om!* Reality (*oṁ satyam oṁ satyam oṁ satyam*).

*Here ends the Artharvaśira Upaniṣad*

## NOTES

[1] Rudra, personification of the principial or causal Entity, is the origin of manifestation. Every reference to Rudra is intended to refer to the ontological state.

[2] *Brahmā* penetrates all things. These are his accidental modifications and they constitute its shadows/lights or its continuum/discontinuum.

The distinction between the unmanifest and the manifest should not be considered as an opposition because the manifest (the shadows/lights) is nothing but the development from the potential state of the unmanifest.

[3] *Bhūḥ, bhuvaḥ, svaḥ* constitute the threefold existential sphere: earth (*bhūmi*), inter-stellar space or intermediate space (*bhuvaḥ*), sky or celestial world of the informal light (*svaḥ*) and, by analogy, the threefold aspects of the constitution of the individual. Every traditional doctrine possesses this tripartition of the macro and microcosm.

[4] *Soma* intended in the sense of the philosophical stone.

[5] The *Puruṣa* preexists light, which is the first differentiation of the primordial Sound.

[6] The great Architect of the universe. The Builder of the universal Temple.

[7] *Om* as principial sound.

[8] Here are represented the unfolding of the subtle primordial energies that give origin to the gross manifestation and their reabsorption into the principial Unity.

[9] See *Ṛg Veda* VII.XXXII.22.

[10] From the condition of the Unmanifest there irradiated the principial Unity, holder of the Principle in its phase of development.

[11] It can be said that the appearance/phenomenon disappears from the screen of Rudra, like a dream disappears from the mental screen on awakening.

[12] The true profound Peace can be realized in the principial Unity, where all traces of polarity vanish. Behind the changing scene of the formal life the ever inalterable Unity exists, in Bliss.

[13] Its polarity, *śakti*, substance of all perishable things, leads the being from birth to death and vice versa.

[14] The *Upaniṣad* highlights the effect of the sound *Aum*. The science of rhythm leads the individualized soul gradually to the Silence of the universal Principle.

[15] 'The Lord (*Īśa*) supports this universe which is the connection between the changeable and the Unchangeable,

of the manifest and of the Unmanifest. The *ātmā*, not independent, is rendered conditioned by the conviction of being the experiencer (*bhoktṛ*). Realizing the *Deva* [the Supreme *ātman*], [the *jīva*] is liberated from all bonds.'[1]

16 The Sound reverts to the principial state.

'Then, elsewhere, it has also been said: Two are, in truth the [different aspects of] *Brahman* on which it should be meditated: that with sound (*śabda*) and that without sound (*aśabda*). Therefore, precisely through that with sound, that without sound is revealed. Now, in this context the sound is [the sacred syllable *Om*.] Ascending to the heights through such [sound] one resolves oneself in the without sound. After which [it is recognized that] undoubtedly this is the way, this is immortality, this is the perfect identity and, similarly, the total pacification.'[2]

In other works, the *Aum* was explained as composed of three *mātras*. Also approached were *nirguṇa Brahman* and *saguṇa Brahman* (according to the metaphysical or the ontological point of view of *Vedānta*) in that principial Point (*bindu*).

Now an additional development to the *Aum* as spatial Entity is given: 'Rudra... is also the space... you are... the extension.'[3]

It can be said, synthetically, that the principial Point, *reflecting itself* or objectifying itself by *polarization* (therefore, not by subdividing itself or by fractionating itself so as to

[1] *Śvetāśvatara Upaniṣad* I.8.

[2] *Maitry Upaniṣad* VI.22.

[3] Cf. *Atharvaśira Upaniṣad* II.24 and III.

lose its particular nature), it determines itself in two points or vortices that are represented by A and U.

This polarization, though, is not outside of the Point, but within it. The Point, which is the Unlimited, cannot obviously go out of itself. The two elementary points/vortices are, therefore, distanced by an *interval*, and it is the latter that brings them into evidence. The interval represents the extension or informal spatial condition, base and support, of every formal expression.

We therefore have that M represents the interval, the connection or primordial spatial relationship of A with U:

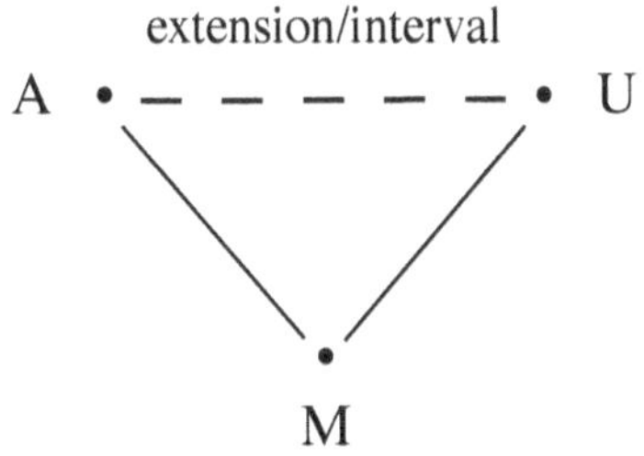


From this it becomes clear that the two points, which position themselves, so to speak, one in front of the other, produce the phenomenon of distance, of extension and therefore of space. These three elements constitute the unmanifest sacred Triad from which everything proceeds.

The space is the son of the Father/Mother who have become active. The *puruṣa* and the *prakṛti* of the *Sāṁkhya*, having become dynamic, produce space/life.

In its turn, (as seen from the empirical point of view), the unlimited abstract existence, or pre-genetic substance under the law of vibration, and therefore of sound/light, is modified into *definite* lengths; in other terms, it is conditioned into determined forms. A body form, therefore, represents a particular delimitation of the unlimited, informal extension. With its movement, a solid delimits a finite contour of space. Under this perspective, a 'plane' has a meaning different from the habitually accepted one that is given to this term; it is something more. All the data are endowed of vibratory movement, and the *grades* of the various vibrations, give precise relationships of measure on that same vibratory scale. These relationships constitute different 'planes.' Every plane is thus determined by the intensity of the same vibrations and by the rhythm with which they are accomplished. The great universal Musician hits the 'keyboard' of the *prakṛti* (*Nu* for the Egyptians) producing *music*, therefore 'qualified planes.'

Everything can be recapitulated in this sequence:

– noumenal Point

– polarized vortices

– informal extension

– indefinite bodies/forms delimiting the principial extension

This implies that every form/body (individual being, planet, star, etc.) fluctuates and floats in the unlimited spacial extension, in the ocean of true life and it constitutes its product and its effect.

All the living form/bodies are movement and are daughters of the space, in it they emerge, grow and are extinguished.

There is, therefore, the substance/Space, unlimited and external to the form; and the space which is finite, limited, internal, exalted and governed by the rhythm of the particular formal contour.

When the external space and the one internal to the form, when the unlimited and the limited, when the even and the odd, are all perfectly commensurate, then the Harmony/*Om* is revealed, and its harmonics resound integral fullness.

The space, as we have seen, expresses the relationship of two points; rather, it can be said that there are no longer points forming a line – the point finding itself devoid of dimension, extension and therefore form, cannot produce any line – but rather it is the *distance*, even if elementary, between the two points.

The extension is the first determination of the Being in that principial Point and the 'measure of everything' to come. The space is thus permeated by the intrinsic quality of the being/Point, and therefore it constitutes its potential and virtual primigenial Harmony (this from the point of view of the individual beings), which must be expressed and manifested, precisely, by the vital forms constructed according to right relations. The empirical human being, for instance, who is of the nature of space and therefore of time, can express itself in rhythms of accord (right *mātra*) or dis-harmonically, depending on whether he is able, or not, to grasp the harmonic measure of the unlimited Space.

The space, presupposes the point and not vice versa, and, if one wants to look at things from the pure metaphysical vision, only the principial Point has value and reality, because the extension, as we have already seen, belongs to the plane of determinations.

If the space is the origin of multiplicity and formal differentiation, these do not invalidate even minimally the principial Point, which is beyond any relation/distance, since it precisely constitutes the supreme causing principle. The dissolution of the spatial construct with its multiplicity and its relationships of accords, in fact, implies the reabsorption of the possible projected points into the principial Point, and, as a consequence, the vanishing of the distances/extensions (this always observed from the individualized visual perspective) and of that which lives within it. Thus, the *image* of the triangle disappears when the three points – that form the real vertices, the natural substratum and the perfect measure – are reabsorbed into a single point.

If it can be stated once more that, if one considers the Space as the Entity containing the indefinite and possible formal unfolding, then it can be identified with the universal Being, as non-formal principle of a particular, determined and geometricized Plane of universal life. The *Aum* is the noumenic 'meter', the measure, and all the things within its delimitation are related to such measure.

But the space, beyond being measure/relation/movement and quantity, is also quality, as has been touched upon earlier, because every movement/sound is qualified. It can rather be said that approaching the One/point, one is within the pure quality/identity, while moving away from it one is within quantity. This also explains the condition of the present cycle which, finding itself very far from the principial Point, exteriorizes more as quantity than as quality.

It is logical to transpose to a qualitative level what was said regarding the spatial quantities. Then one has the following configuration which can take also the symbology of the Cross (quantity/quality).

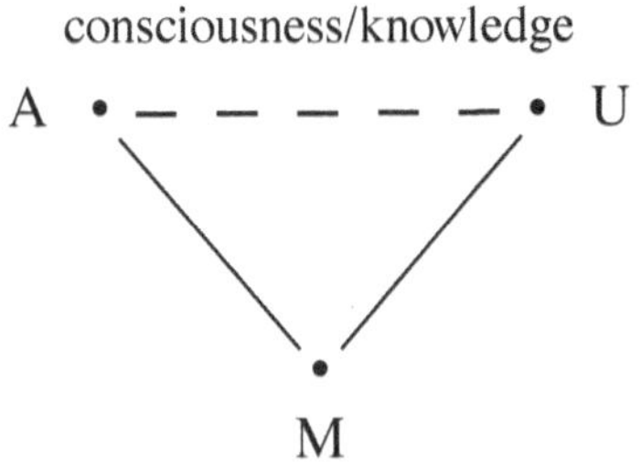


A, subject; U, object; M, consciousness/knowledge

Consciousness constitutes the means that puts subject and object in relationship. It is the third factor which, at a qualitative level, assumes the same functions of the extended entity demonstrated earlier.

This is valid for knowledge (where we have the being polarizing into the object and subject of knowledge) and for other spatial qualifications such as Love, as the instrument of relationship and of union, etc. But the three elements (A U M), with whatever expression one wishes to compare them, are nothing but the principial One point. Therefore it can be said that the Being, through the Being, reveals the Being, or to use a terminology of Islamic esotericism: 'Allah has created the world from Himself through Himself in Himself;' 'He has sent his message from Himself to Himself through Himself.'

'*Oṁ*. That is Fullness this is fullness
Fullness derives from Fullness
Drawing fullness from Fullness
What remains is still Fullness.'[1]

[1] *Īśa Upaniṣad Invocation*.

17 'In the sublime golden involucre is *Brahman*, without impurities and devoid of parts: That is perfectly clear, it is the light of lights. That is what the knowers of the *ātman* realize.'[1]

18 One who has been able to reduce substance into essence, has found the principial Harmony. One who has transcended this last state has revealed the supreme *Brahman*. This is the vision of the *Vedānta*.

---

[1] *Muṇḍaka Upaniṣad* II.II.9.

SANSKRIT TEXT

# īśāvāsyopaniṣat

pūrṇamadaḥ pūrṇamidaṁ pūrṇātpūrṇamudacyate ।
pūrṇasya pūrṇamādāya pūrṇamevāvaśiṣyate ॥

oṁ śāntiḥ śāntiḥ śāntiḥ

īśā vāsyamidaṁ sarvaṁ yatkiñca jagatyāṁ jagat ।
tena tyaktena bhuñjīthā mā gṛdhaḥ kasyasviddhanam ॥ 1 ॥

kurvanneveha karmāṇi jijıviṣecchataṁ samāḥ ।
evaṁ tvayi nānyatheto 'na karma lipyate nare ॥ 2 ॥

asuryā nāma te lokā andhena tamasāvṛtāḥ ।
tāṁste pretyābhigacchanti ye ke cātmahano janāḥ ॥ 3 ॥

anejadekaṁ manaso javīyo nainaddevā āpnuvanpūrvamarṣat ।
taddhāvato 'nyānatyeti tiṣṭhattasminnāpo mātariśvā dadhāti ॥ 4 ॥

tadejati tannaijati taddūre tadvantike ।
tadantarasya sarvasya tadu sarvasyāsya bāhyataḥ ॥ 5 ॥

yastu sarvāṇi bhūtānyātmanyevānupaśyati ।
sarvabhūteṣu cātmānaṁ tato na vijugupsate ॥ 6 ॥

yasminsarvāṇi bhūtānyātmaivābhūdvijānataḥ ।
tatra ko mohaḥ kaḥ śoka ekatvamanupaśyataḥ ॥ 7 ॥

sa paryagācchukramakāyamavraṇam
asnāviraṁ śuddhamapāpaviddham ।

kavirmanīṣī paribhūḥ svayambhūryāthātathyato
'rthānvyadadhācchāśvatībhyaḥ samābhyaḥ ॥ 8 ॥

andhantamaḥ praviśanti ye 'vidyāmupāsate ।
tato bhūya iva te tato ya u vidyāyāṁ ratāḥ ॥ 9 ॥

anyadevāhurvidyayānyadāhuravidyayā ।
iti śuśruma dhīrāṇāṁ ye nastadvicacakṣire ॥ 10 ॥
vidyāṁ cāvidyāṁ ca yastadvedobhayaṁ saha ।
avidyayā mṛtyuṁ tīrtvā vidyayāmṛtamaśnute ॥ 11 ॥

andhaṁ tamaḥ praviśanti ye 'sambhūtimupāsate ।
tato bhūya iva te tamo ya u sambhūtyāṁ ratāḥ ॥ 12 ॥

anyadevāhuḥ sambhavādanyadāhurasambhavāt ।
iti śuśruma dhīrāṇāṁ ye nastadvicacakṣire ॥ 13 ॥

sambhūtiṁ ca vināśaṁ ca yastadvedobhayaṁ saha ।
vināśena mṛtyuṁ tīrtvā sambhūtyāmṛtamaśnute ॥ 14 ॥

hiraṇmayena pātreṇa satyasyāpihitaṁ mukham ।
tattvaṁ pūṣannapāvṛṇu satyadharmāya dṛṣṭaye ॥ 15 ॥

pūṣannekarṣe yama sūrya
prājāpatya vyūha raśmīnsamūha ।
tejo yatte rūpaṁ kalyāṇatamaṁ tatte
paśyāmi yo 'sāvasau puruṣaḥ so 'hamasmi ॥ 16 ॥

vāyuranilamamṛtamathedaṁ bhasmāntaṁ śarīram ।
oṁkrato smara kṛtaṁ smara krato smara kṛtaṁ smara ॥ 17 ॥

agne naya supathā rāye asmān viśvāni deva vayunāni vidvān ।
yuyodhyasmajjuhurāṇameno bhūyiṣṭhāṁ te nama uktiṁ
vidhema ॥ 18 ॥

iti īśāvāsyopaniṣatsamāptā

# kaivalyopaniṣat

harih oṁ |

oṁ yathāśvalāyano bhagavantaṁ
  parameṣṭhinamupasametyovāca |
adhīhi bhagavanbrahmavidyāṁ variṣṭhāṁ
  sadā sadbhiḥ sevyamānāṁ nigūḍhām |
yathā 'cirātsarvapāpaṁ vyapohya
  parātparaṁ puruṣaṁ yāti vidvān || 1 ||

tasmai sa hovāca pitāmahaśca śraddhābhaktidhyānayogādavaihi |
na karmaṇā na prajayā dhanena tyāgenaike 'mṛtatvamānaśuḥ || 2 ||

pareṇa nākaṁ nihitaṁ guhāyāṁ
  vibhrājate yadyatayo viśanti |
vedāntavijñānasuniścitārthāḥ
  saṁnyāsayogādyatayaḥ śuddhasattvāḥ || 3 ||

te brahmalokeṣu parāntakāle parāmṛtāḥ parimucyanti sarve || 4 ||

viviktadeśe ca sukhāsanasthaḥ
  śuciḥ samagrīvaśiraḥśarīraḥ |
antyāśramasthaḥ sakalendriyāṇi
  nirudhya bhaktyā svaguruṁ praṇamya |
hṛtpuṇḍarīkaṁ virajaṁ viśuddhaṁ
  vicintya madhye viśadaṁ viśokam || 5 ||

acintyamavyaktamanantarūpaṁ
    śivaṁ praśāntamamṛtaṁ brahmayonim |

tamādimadhyāntavihīnamekaṁ
vibhuṁ cidānandamarūpamadbhūtam || 6 ||

umāsahāyaṁ parameśvaraṁ prabhuṁ
trilocanaṁ nīlakaṇṭhaṁ praśāntam |
dhyātvā munirgacchati bhūtayoniṁ
samastasākṣiṁ tamasaḥ parastāt || 7 ||

sa brahmā sa śivaḥ sendraḥ so 'kṣaraḥ paramaḥ svarāṭ |
sa eva viṣṇuḥ sa prāṇaḥ sa kālo 'gniḥ sa candramāḥ || 8 ||

sa eva sarvaṁ yadbhūtaṁ yacca bhavyaṁ sanātanam |
jñātvā taṁ mṛtyumatyeti nānyaḥ panthā vimuktaye || 9 ||

sarvabhūtasthamātmānaṁ sarvabhūtāni cātmani |
saṁpaśyanbrahma paramaṁ yāti nānyena hetunā || 10 ||

ātmānamaraṇiṁ kṛtvā praṇavaṁ cottarāraṇim |
jñānanirmathanābhyāsātpāpaṁ dahati paṇḍitaḥ || 11 ||

sa eva māyāparimohitātmā śarīramāsthāya karoti sarvam |
striyannapānādivicitrabhogaiḥ sa eva jāgratparitṛptimeti || 12 ||

svapne sa jīvaḥ sukhaduḥkhabhoktā
svamāyayā kalpitajīvaloke |
suṣuptikāle sakale vilīne
tamo 'bhibhūtaḥ sukharūpameti ||
punaśca janmāntarakarmayogāt |
sa eva jīvaḥ svapati prabuddhaḥ || 13 ||

puratraye krīḍati yaśca jīvas
tataḥ sujātaṁ sakalaṁ vicitram |
ādhāramānandamakhaṇḍabodhaṁ
yasmiṁllayaṁ yāti puratrayaṁ ca || 14 ||

etasmājjāyate prāṇo manaḥ sarvendriyāṇi ca |
khaṁ vāyurjyotirāpaśca pṛthvī viśvasya dhāriṇī || 15 ||

yatparaṁ brahma sarvātmā viśvasyāyatanaṁ mahat |
sūkṣmātsūkṣmataraṁ nityaṁ sa tvameva tvameva tat || 16 ||

jāgratsvapnasuṣuptyādiprapañcaṁ yatprakāśate ।
tadbrahmāhamiti jñātvā sarvabandhaiḥ pramucyate ॥ 17 ॥

triṣu dhāmasu yadbhogyaṁ bhoktā bhogaśca yadbhavet ।
tebhyo vilakṣaṇaḥ sākṣī cinmātro 'haṁ sadāśivaḥ ॥ 18 ॥

mayyeva sakalaṁ jātaṁ mayi sarvaṁ pratiṣṭhitam ।
mayi sarvaṁ layaṁ yāti tadbrahmādvayamasmyaham ॥ 19 ॥

aṇoranīyānahameva tadvan
mahānahaṁviśvamahaṁ vicitram ।
purātano 'haṁ puruṣo 'hamīśo
hiraṇmayo 'haṁ śivarūpamasmi ॥ 20 ॥

apāṇipādo 'hamacintyaśaktiḥ
paśyāmyacakṣuḥ sa śṛṇomyakarṇaḥ ।
ahaṁ vijānāmi viviktarūpo
na cāsti vettā mama citsadāham ।
vedairanekairahameva vedyo
vedāntakṛdvedavideva cāham ॥ 21 ॥

na puṇyapāpe mama nāsti nāśo
na janma dehendriyabuddhirasti ।
na bhūmirāpo na ca vahnirasti
na cānilo me 'sti na cāmbaraṁ ca ॥ 22 ॥

evaṁ viditvā paramātmarūpaṁ
guhāśayaṁ niṣkalamadvitīyam ।
samastasākṣiṁ sadasadvihīnaṁ
prayāti śuddhaṁ paramātmarūpam ॥ 23 ॥

iti kaivalyopaniṣatsamāptā

## sarvasāropaniṣat

kathaṁ bandhaḥ kathaṁ mokṣaḥ kā vidyā kā 'vidyeti | jāgratsvapnasuṣuptiturīyaṁ ca katham | annamayaprāṇamayamanomayavijñānamayānandamayakośāḥ katham | kartā jīvaḥ pañcavargaḥ kṣetrajñaḥ sākṣī kūṭastho 'ntaryāmī katham | pratyagātmā parātmā māyā ceti katham | ātmeśvarajīvaḥ anātmanāṁ dehādīnāmātmatvenābhimanyate so 'bhimāna ātmano bandhaḥ | tannivṛttirmokṣaḥ | yā tadabhimānaṁ kārayati sā avidyā | so 'bhimāno yayā nivartate sā vidyā | manaādicaturdaśakaraṇaiḥ puṣkalairādityādyanugṛhītaiḥ śabdādīnviṣayānsthūlānyadopalabhate tadātmano jāgaraṇam | tadvāsanāsahitaiścaturdaśakaraṇaiḥ śabdādyabhāve 'pi vāsanāmayāñchabdādīnyadopalabhate tadātmanaḥ svapnam | caturdaśakaraṇoparamādviśeṣavijñānābhāvādyadā śabdādīnnopalabhate tadātmanaḥ suṣuptam | avasthātrayabhāvābhāvasākṣī svayaṁbhāvarahitaṁ nairantaryaṁ caitanyaṁ yadā tadā turīyaṁ caitanyamityucyate | annakāryāṇāṁ kośānāṁ samūho 'nnamayaḥ kośa ityucyate | prāṇādicaturdaśavāyubhedā annamayakośe yadā vartante tadā prāṇamayaḥ kośa ityucyate | etatkośadvayasaṁsaktaṁ manaādicaturdaśakaraṇairātmā śabdādiviṣayasaṅkalpādīndharmānyadā karoti tadā manomayaḥ kośa ityucyate | etatkośatrayasaṁsaktaṁ tadgataviśeṣajño yadā bhāsate tadā vijñānamayaḥ kośa ityucyate | etatkośacatuṣṭayaṁ saṁsaktaṁ svakāraṇājñāne vaṭakāṇikāyāmiva vṛkṣo yadā vartate tadānandamayaḥ kośa ityucyate | sukhaduḥkhabuddhyā śreyo 'ntaḥ kartā yadā tadā iṣṭaviṣaye buddhiḥ sukhabuddhiraniṣṭaviṣaye buddhirduḥkhabuddhiḥ | śabdasparśarūparasagandhāḥ sukhaduḥkhahetavaḥ | puṇyapāpakarmānusārī bhūtvā prāptaśarīrasaṁyogamaprāptaśarīrasaṁyogamiva kurvāṇo yadā dṛśyate tadopahitajīva ityucyate | manaādiśca prāṇādiścecchādiśca sattvādiśca puṇyādiścaite pañcavargā ityeteṣāṁ pañcavargāṇāṁ dharmībhūtātmā jñānādṛte na vinaśyatyātmasannidhau nityatvena pratīyamāna ātmopādhiryastalliṅgaśarīraṁ hṛdgranthirityucyate tatra yatprakāśate caitanyaṁ sa kṣetrajña ityucyate । jñātṛjñānajñeyānāmāvirbhāvatirobhāvajñātā svayamāvirbhāvatirobhāvarahitaḥ svayaṁjyotiḥ sākṣītyucyate । brahmādipipīlikāparyantaṁ sarvaprāṇibuddhiṣvavaśiṣṭatayopalabhyamānaḥ sarvaprāṇibuddhistho yadā tadā kūṭastha ityucyate । kūṭasthopahitabhedānāṁ svarūpalābhaheturbhūtvā maṇigaṇe sūtramiva sarvakṣetreṣvanusyūtatvena yadā kāśyate ātmā tadāntaryāmītyucyate । satyaṁ jñānamanantamānandaṁ sarvopādhivinirmuktaṁ kaṭakamukuṭādyupādhirahitasuvarṇaghanavadvijñānacinmātrasvabhāvātmā yadā bhāsate tadā tvaṁpadārthaḥ । satyaṁ jñānamanantaṁ brahma । satyamavināśi । avināśi nāma deśakālavastunimitteṣu vinaśyatsu yanna vinaśyati tadavināśi । jñānaṁ nāmotpattivināśarahitaṁ nairantaryaṁ caitanyaṁ jñānamityucyate । anantaṁ nāma mṛdvikāreṣu mṛdiva svarṇavikāreṣu svarṇamiva tantuvikāreṣu tanturivāvyaktādisṛṣṭiprapañceṣu pūrṇaṁ vyāpakaṁ caitanyamanantamityucyate । ānandaṁ nāma sukhacaitanyasvarūpo 'parimitānandasamudro 'vaśiṣṭasukhasvarūpaścānanda ityucyate । etadvastucatuṣṭayaṁ yasya lakṣaṇaṁ deśakālavastunimitteṣvavyabhicārī tatpadārthaḥ paramātmetyucyate । tvaṁpadārthādaupādhikāttatpadārthādaupādhikabhedādvilakṣaṇamākāśavatsūkṣmaṁ kevalasattāmātrasvabhāvaṁ paraṁ brahmetyucyate । māyā nāma anādirantavatī pramāṇāpramāṇasādhāraṇā na satī nāsatī na sadasatī svayamadhikā vikārarahitā nirūpyamāṇā satītaralakṣaṇaśūnyā sā māyetyucyate । nāhaṁ bhavāmyahaṁ devo nendriyāṇi daśaiva tu ॥

na buddhirna manaḥ śaśvannāhaṅkārastathaiva ca ॥ 1 ॥

aprāṇo hyamanāḥ śubhro buddhyādīnāṁ hi sarvadā ।
sākṣyahaṁ sarvadā nityaścinmātro 'haṁ na saṁśayaḥ ॥ 2 ॥

nāhaṁ kartā naiva bhoktā prakṛteḥ sākṣirūpakaḥ ।
matsānnidhyātpravartante dehādyā aja*f*ā iva ॥ 3 ॥

sthāṇurnityaḥ sadānandaḥ śuddho jñānamayo 'malaḥ ।
ātmāhaṁ sarvabhūtānāṁ vibhuḥ sākṣī na saṁśayaḥ ॥ 4 ॥

brahmaivāhaṁ sarvavedāntavedyaṁ
nāhaṁ vedyaṁ vyomavātādirūpam ।
rūpaṁ nāhaṁ nāma nāhaṁ na karma
brahmaivāhaṁ saccidānandarūpam ॥ 5 ॥

nāhaṁ deho janmamṛtyū kuto me
  nāhaṁ prāṇaḥ kṣutpipāse kuto me |
nāhaṁ cetaḥ śokamohau kuto me
  nāhaṁ kartā bandhamokṣau kuto me || 6 ||

iti sarvasāropaniṣatsamāptā

## amṛtabindūpaniṣat

mano hi dvividhaṁ proktaṁ śuddhaṁ cāśuddhameva ca |
aśuddhaṁ kāmasaṅkalpaṁ śuddhaṁ kāmavivarjitam || 1 ||

mana eva manuṣyāṇāṁ kāraṇaṁ bandhamokṣayoḥ |
bandhāya viṣayāsaktaṁ muktyai nirviṣayaṁ smṛtam || 2 ||

yato nirviṣayasyāsya manaso muktiriṣyate |
tasmānnirviṣayaṁ nityaṁ manaḥ kāryaṁ mumukṣuṇā || 3 ||

nirastaviṣayāsaṅgaṁ saṁniruddhaṁ mano hṛdi |
yadā yātyunmanībhāvaṁ tadā tatparamaṁ padam || 4 ||

tāvadeva niroddhavyaṁ yāvaddhṛdi gataṁ kṣayam |
etajjñānaṁ ca mokṣaṁ ca ato 'nyo granthavistaraḥ || 5 ||

naiva cintyaṁ na cācintyamacintyaṁ cintyameva ca |
pakṣapātavinirmuktaṁ brahma saṁpadyate tadā || 6 ||

svareṇa saṁdhayedyogamasvaraṁ bhāvayetparam |
asvareṇa hi bhāvena bhāvo nābhāva iṣyate || 7 ||

tadeva niṣkalaṁ brahma nirvikalpaṁ nirañjanam |
tadbrahmāhamiti jñātvā brahma saṁpadyate dhruvam || 8 ||

nirvikalpamanantaṁ ca hetudṛṣṭāntavarjitam |
aprameyamanādyaṁ ca jñātvā ca paramaṁ śivam || 9 ||

na nirodho na cotpattirna vandyo na ca śāsanam |
na mumukṣā na muktiśca ityeṣā paramārthatā || 10 ||

eka evātmā mantavyo jāgratsvapnasuṣuptiṣu ।
sthānatrayādvyatītasya punarjanma na vidyate ॥ 11 ॥

eka eva hi bhūtātmā bhūte bhūte vyavasthitaḥ ।
ekadhā bahudhā caiva dṛśyate jalacandravat ॥ 12 ॥

ghaṭasaṁbhṛtamākāśaṁ līyamāne ghaṭe yathā ।
ghaṭo līyeta nākāśaṁ tadvajjīvo ghaṭopamaḥ ॥ 13 ॥

ghaṭavadvividhākāraṁ bhidyamānaṁ punaḥ punaḥ ।
tadbhagnaṁ na ca jānāti sa jānāti ca nityaśaḥ ॥ 14 ॥

śabdamāyāvṛto yāvattāvattiṣṭhati puṣkare ।
bhinne tamasi caikatvamekamevānupaśyati ॥ 15 ॥

śabdākṣaraṁ paraṁ brahma yasminkṣīṇe yadakṣaram ।
tadvidvānakṣaraṁ dhyāyedyadīcchecchāntimātmanaḥ ॥ 16 ॥

dve vidye veditavye tu śabdabrahma paraṁ ca yat ।
śabdabrahmaṇi niṣṇātaḥ paraṁ brahmādhigacchati ॥ 17 ॥

granthamabhyasya medhāvī jñānavijñānatattvataḥ ।
palālamiva dhānyārthī tyajedgranthamaśeṣataḥ ॥ 18 ॥

gavāmanekavarṇānāṁ kṣīrasyāpyekavarṇatā ।
kṣīravatpaśyate jñānaṁ liṅginastu gavāṁ yathā ॥ 19 ॥

ghṛtamiva payasi nigū*f*haṁ bhūte bhūte ca vasati vijñānam ।
satataṁ manthayitavyaṁ manasā manthānabhūtena ॥ 20 ॥

jñānanetraṁ samādāya caredvahnimataḥ param ।
niṣkalaṁ nirmalaṁ śāntaṁ tadbrahmāhamiti smṛtam ॥ 21 ॥

sarvabhūtādhivāsaṁ ca yadbhūteṣu vasatyadhi ।
sarvānugrāhakatvena tadasmyahaṁ vāsudevaḥ
tadasmyahaṁ vāsudeva iti ॥ 22 ॥

iti amṛtabindūpaniṣatsamāptā

# atharvaśiropaniṣat

oṁ devā ha vai svargaṁ lokamāyaṁste rudramapṛcchanko bhavāniti | so 'bravīdahamekaḥ prathamamāsaṁ vartāmi ca bhaviṣyāmi ca nānyaḥ kaścinmatto vyatirikta iti | so 'ntarādantaraṁ prāviśaddiścaścāntaraṁ prāviśatso 'haṁ nityānityo 'haṁ vyaktāvyakto brahmābrahmāhaṁ prāñcaḥ pratyañco 'haṁ dakṣiṇāñca udañco 'haṁ adhaścordhvaṁ cāhaṁ diśaśca pratidiśaścāhaṁ pumānapumānstriyaścāhaṁ gāyatryahaṁ sāvitryahaṁ triṣṭubjagatyanuṣṭupcāhaṁ chando 'haṁ gārhapatyo dakṣiṇāgnirāhavanīyo 'haṁ satyo 'haṁ gaurahaṁ gauryahamṛgahaṁ yajurahaṁ sāmāhamatharvāṅgiraso 'haṁ jyeṣṭho 'haṁ śreṣṭho 'haṁ variṣṭho 'hamāpo 'haṁ tejo 'haṁ guhyo 'hamaraṇyo 'hamakṣaramahaṁ kṣaramahaṁ puṣkaramahaṁ pavitramahamugraṁ ca madhyaṁ ca bahiśca purastājjyotirityahameva sarvebhyo māmeva sa sarvaḥ samāṁ yo māṁ veda sa sarvāndevānveda sarvāṁśca devānsāṅgānapi brahma brāhmaṇaiśca gāṁ gobhirbrāhmaṇānbrāhmaṇena havirhaviṣā āyurāyuṣā satyena satyaṁ dharmeṇa dharmaṁ tarpayāmi svena tejasā | tato ha vai te devā rudramapṛcchante devā rudramapaśyan | te devā rudramadhyāyantato devā ūrdhvabāhavo rudraṁ stuvanti || **1** ||

oṁ yo vai rudraḥ sa bhagavānyaśca brahmā tasmai vai namonamaḥ || 1 ||

yo vai rudraḥ sa bhagavānyaśca viṣṇustasmai vai namonamaḥ || 2 ||

yo vai rudraḥ sa bhagavānyaśca skandastasmai vai namonamaḥ || 3 ||

yo vai rudraḥ sa bhagavānyaścendrastasmai vai namonamaḥ || 4 ||

yo vai rudraḥ sa bhagavānyaścāgnistasmai vai namonamaḥ || 5 ||

yo vai rudraḥ sa bhagavānyaśca vāyustasmai vai namonamaḥ || 6 ||

yo vai rudraḥ sa bhagavānyaśca sūryastasmai vai namonamaḥ || 7 ||

yo vai rudraḥ sa bhagavānyaśca somastasmai vai namonamaḥ ॥ 8 ॥

yo vai rudraḥ sa bhagavānyo cāṣṭo grahāstasmai vai namonamaḥ ॥ 9 ॥

yo vai rudraḥ sa bhagavānyo cāṣṭo pratigrahāstasmai vai namonamaḥ ॥ 10 ॥

yo vai rudraḥ sa bhagavānyacca bhūstasmai vai namonamaḥ ॥ 11 ॥

yo vai rudraḥ sa bhagavānyacca bhuvastasmai vai namonamaḥ ॥ 12 ॥

yo vai rudraḥ sa bhagavānyacca svastasmai vai namonamaḥ ॥ 13 ॥

yo vai rudraḥ sa bhagavānyacca mahastasmai vai namonamaḥ ॥ 14 ॥

yo vai rudraḥ sa bhagavānyā ca pṛthvī tasmai vai namonamaḥ ॥ 15 ॥

yo vai rudraḥ sa bhagavānyaccāntarikṣaṁ tasmai vai namonamaḥ ॥ 16 ॥

yo vai rudraḥ sa bhagavānyā ca dyaustasmai vai namonamaḥ ॥ 17 ॥

yo vai rudraḥ sa bhagavānyāścāpastasmai vai namonamaḥ ॥ 18 ॥

yo vai rudraḥ sa bhagavānyacca tejastasmai vai namonamaḥ ॥ 19 ॥

yo vai rudraḥ sa bhagavānyaśca kālastasmai vai namonamaḥ ॥ 20 ॥

yo vai rudraḥ sa bhagavānyaścayamastasmai vai namonamaḥ ॥ 21 ॥

yo vai rudraḥ sa bhagavānyaśca mṛtyustasmai vai namonamaḥ ॥ 22 ॥

yo vai rudraḥ sa bhagavānyaccāmṛtaṁ tasmai vai namonamaḥ ॥ 23 ॥

yo vai rudraḥ sa bhagavānyaccākāśaṁ tasmai vai namonamaḥ ॥ 24 ॥

yo vai rudraḥ sa bhagavānyacca viśvaṁ tasmai vai namonamaḥ ॥ 25 ॥

yo vai rudraḥ sa bhagavānyacca sthūlaṁ tasmai vai namonamaḥ ॥ 26 ॥

yo vai rudraḥ sa bhagavānyacca sūkṣmaṁ tasmai vai namonamaḥ ॥ 27 ॥

yo vai rudraḥ sa bhagavānyacca śuklaṁ tasmai vai namonamaḥ ॥ 28 ॥

yo vai rudraḥ sa bhagavānyacca kṛṣṇaṁ tasmai vai namonamaḥ ॥ 29 ॥

yo vai rudraḥ sa bhagavānyacca kṛtsnaṁ tasmai vai namonamaḥ ॥ 30 ॥

yo vai rudraḥ sa bhagavānyacca satyaṁ tasmai vai namonamaḥ ॥ 31 ॥

yo vai rudraḥ sa bhagavānyacca sarvaṁ tasmai vai namonamaḥ ॥ 32 ॥ **2** ॥

bhūste ādirmadhyaṁ bhuvaḥ svaste śīrṣaṁ viśvarūpo 'si brahmaikastvaṁ dvidhā tridhā vṛddhistvaṁ śāntistvaṁ puṣṭistvaṁ hutamahutaṁ dattamadattaṁ sarvamasarvaṁ viśvamaviśvaṁ kṛtamakṛtaṁ paramaparaṁ parāyaṇaṁ ca tvam | apāma somamamṛtā abhūmāganma jyotiravidāma devān | kiṁ nūnamasmānkṛṇavadarātiḥ kimu dhūrtiramṛtaṁ mārtyasya | somasūryapurastātsūkṣmaḥ puruṣaḥ | sarvaṁ jagaddhitaṁ vā etadakṣaraṁ prājāpatyaṁ sūkṣmaṁ saumyaṁ puruṣaṁ grāhyamagrāhyeṇa bhāvaṁ bhāvena saumyaṁ saumyena sūkṣmaṁ sūkṣmeṇa vāyavyaṁ vāyavyena grasati svena tejasā tasmādupasaṁhartre vai namo namaḥ | hṛdisthā devatāḥ sarvā hṛdi prāṇāḥ pratiṣṭhitāḥ | hṛdi tvamasi yo nityaṁ tisro mātrāḥ parastu saḥ | tasyottarataḥ śiro dakṣiṇataḥ pādau ya uttarataḥ sa oṁkāraḥ ya oṁkāraḥ sa praṇavaḥ yaḥ praṇavaḥ sa sarvavyāpī yaḥ sarvavyāpī so 'nantaḥ yo 'nantastattāraṁ yattāraṁ tatsūkṣmaṁ yatsūkṣmaṁ tacchuklaṁ yacchuklaṁ tadvaidyutaṁ yadvaidyutaṁ tatparaṁ brahma yatparaṁ brahma sa ekaḥ ya ekaḥ sa rudraḥ yo rudraḥ sa īśānaḥ ya īśānaḥ sa bhagavānmaheśvaraḥ || **3** ||

atha kasmāducyata oṁkāro yasmāduccāryamāṇa eva prāṇānūrdhvamutkrāmayati tasmāducyate oṁkāraḥ | atha kasmāducyate praṇavaḥ yasmāduccāryamāṇa eva ṛgyajuḥsāmātharvāṅgirasaṁ brahma brāhmaṇebhyaḥ praṇāmayati nāmayati ca tasmāducyate praṇavaḥ | atha kasmāducyate sarvavyāpī yasmāduccāryamāṇa eva sarvāṁllokānvyāpnoti sneho yathā palalapiṇ*f*amiva śāntarūpamotaprotamanuprāpto vyatiṣaktaśca tasmāducyate sarvavyāpī | atha kasmāducyate 'nanto yasmāduccāryamāṇa eva tīryagūrdhvamadhastāccāsyānto nopalabhyate tasmāducyate 'nantaḥ | atha kasmāducyate tāraṁ yasmāduccāryamāṇa eva garbhajanmavyādhijarāmaraṇasaṁsāramahābhayāttārayati trāyate ca tasmāducyate tāram | atha kasmāducyate śuklaṁ yasmāduccāryamāṇa evaklandate klāmayati ca tasmāducyate śuklam | atha kasmāducyate sūkṣmaṁ yasmāduccāryamāṇa eva sūkṣmo bhūtvā śarīrāṇyadhitiṣṭhati sarvāṇi cāṅgānyamimṛśati tasmāducyate sūkṣmam | atha kasmāducyate vaidyutaṁ yasmāduccāryamāṇa eva vyakte mahati tamasi dyotayati tasmāducyate vaidyutam | atha kasmāducyate paraṁ brahma yasmātparamaparaṁ parāyaṇaṁ ca bṛhadbṛhatyā bṛṁhayati tasmāducyate paraṁ brahma | atha kasmāducyate ekaḥ yaḥ sarvānprāṇānsaṁbhakṣya saṁbhakṣaṇenājaḥ saṁsṛjati visṛjati tīrthameke vrajanti tīrthameke dakṣiṇāḥ pratyañca udañcaḥ prāñco 'bhivrajantyeke teṣāṁ sarveṣāmiha sadgatiḥ | sākaṁ sa eko bhūtaścarati prajānāṁ tasmāducyata ekaḥ I atha kasmāducyate rudraḥ yasmādṛṣibhirnānyairbhaktairdrutamasya rūpamupalabhyate tasmāducyate rudraḥ I atha kasmāducyate īśānaḥ yaḥ sarvāndevānīśate īśānībhirjananībhiśca paramaśaktibhiḥ I abhitvā śūra ṇo numo dugdhā iva dhenavaḥ I īśānamasya jagataḥ svardṛśamīśānamindra tasthuṣa iti tasmāducyate īśānaḥ I atha kasmāducyate bhagavānmaheśvaraḥ yasmādbhaktā jñānena bhajantyanugṛhṇāti ca vācaṁ saṁsṛjati visṛjati ca sarvānbhāvānparityajyātmajñānena yogaiśvaryeṇa mahati mahīyate tasmāducyate bhagavānmaheśvaraḥ I tadetadrudracaritam II **4** II

eko ha devaḥ pradiśo nu sarvāḥ pūrvo ha jātaḥ sa u garbhe antaḥ I sa eva jātaḥ janiṣyamāṇaḥ pratyaṅjanāstiṣṭhati sarvatomukhaḥ I eko rudro na dvitīyāya tasmai ya imāṁllokānīśata īśanībhiḥ I pratyaṅjanāstiṣṭhati saṁcukocāntakāle saṁsṛjya viśvā bhuvanāni goptā I yo yoniṁ yonimadhitiṣṭhatityeko yenedaṁ sarvaṁ vicarati sarvam I tamīśānaṁ puruṣaṁ devamī*f*yaṁ nicāyyemāṁ śāntimatyantameti I kṣamāṁ hitvā hetujālāsya mūlaṁ buddhyā saṁcitaṁ sthāpayitvā tu rudre I rudramekatvamāhuḥ śāśvataṁ vai purāṇamiśamūrjeṇa paśavo 'nunāmayantaṁ mṛtyupāśān I tadetenātmannetenārdhacaturthena mātreṇa śāntiṁ saṁsṛjanti paśupāśavimokṣaṇam I yā sā prathamā mātrā brahmadevatyā raktā varṇena yastāṁ dhyāyate nityaṁ sa gacchedbrahmapadam I yā sā dvitīyā mātrā viṣṇudevatyā kṛṣṇā varṇena yastāṁ dhyāyate nityaṁ sa gacchedvaiṣṇavaṁ padam I yā sā tṛtīyā mātrā īśānadevatyā kapilā varṇena yastāṁ dhyāyate nityaṁ sa gacchedaiśānaṁ padam I yā sārdhacaturthī mātrā sarvadevatyā 'vyaktībhūtā khaṁ vicarati śuddhā sphaṭikasannibhā varṇena yastāṁ dhyāyate nityaṁ sa gacchetpadamanāmayam I tadetadupāsīta munayo vāgvadanti na tasya grahaṇamayaṁ panthā vihita uttareṇa yena devā yānti yena pitaro yena ṛṣayaḥ paramaparaṁ parāyaṇaṁ ceti I vālāgramātraṁ hṛdayasya madhye viśvaṁ devaṁ jātarūpaṁ vareṇyam I tamātmasthaṁ yenu paśyanti dhīrāsteṣāṁ śāntirbhavati netareṣām I yasminkrodhaṁ yāṁ ca tṛṣṇaṁ kṣamāṁ cākṣamāṁ hitvā hetujālasya mūlam I buddhyā saṁcitaṁ sthāpayitvā tu rudre rudramekatvamāhuḥ I rudro hi śāśvatena vai purāṇeneṣamūrjeṇa tapasā niyantā I agniriti bhasma vāyuriti bhasma jalamiti bhasma sthalamiti bhasma vyometi bhasma sarvaṁ ha vā idaṁ bhasma mana etāni cakṣūṁṣi yasmādvratamidaṁ pāśupataṁ yadbhasma nāṅgāni saṁspṛśettasmādbrahma tadetatpāśupataṁ paśupāśavimokṣaṇāya II **5** II yo 'gnau rudro yo 'psvantarya oṣadhīrvīrudha āviveśa | ya imā viśvā bhuvanāni cakøpe tasmai rudrāya namo 'stvagnaye | yo rudro 'gnau yo rudro 'psvantaryo rudra oṣadhīrvīrudha āviveśa | yo rudra imā viśvā bhuvanāni cakøpe tasmai rudrāya namonamaḥ | yo rudro 'psu yo rudra oṣadhīṣu yo rudro vanaspatiṣu | yena rudreṇa jagadūrdhvaṁ dhāritaṁ pṛthivī dvidhā tridhā dhartā dhāritā nāgā ye 'ntarikṣe tasmai rudrāya vai namonamaḥ | mūrdhānamasya saṁsevyāpyatharvā hṛdayaṁ ca yat | mastiṣkādūrdhvaṁ prerayatyamāno 'dhiśīrṣataḥ | tadvā atharvaṇaḥ śiro devakośaḥ samujjhitaḥ | tatprāṇo 'bhirakṣati śiro 'ntamatho manaḥ | na ca divo devajanena guptā na cāntarikṣāṇi na ca bhūma imāḥ | yasminnidaṁ sarvamotaprotaṁ tasmādanyanna paraṁ kiṁcanāsti | na tasmātpūrvaṁ na paraṁ tadasti na bhūtaṁ nota bhavyaṁ yadāsıt | sahasrapādekamūrdhnā vyāptaṁ sa evedamāvarīvarti bhūtam | akṣarātsaṁjāyate kālaḥ kālādvyāpaka ucyate | vyāpako hi bhagavānrudro bhogāyamāno yadā śete rudrastadā saṁhāryate prajāḥ | ucchvāsite tamo bhavati tamasa āpo 'psvaṅgulyā mathite mathitaṁ śiśire śiśiraṁ mathyamānaṁ phenaṁ bhavati phenādaṇ*f*aṁ bhavatyaṇ*f*ādbrahmā bhavati brahmaṇo vāyuḥ vāyoroṁkāraḥ oṁkārātsāvitrī sāvitryā gāyatrī gāyatryā lokā bhavanti | arcayanti tapaḥ satyaṁ madhu kṣaranti yadbhuvam | etaddhi paramaṁ tapaḥ | āpojyotī raso 'mṛtaṁ brahma bhūrbhuvaḥ svaro nama iti || **6** ||

ya idamatharvaśiro brāhmaṇo 'dhīte 'śrotriyaḥ śrotriyo bhavatyanupanīta upanīto bhavati so 'gnipūto bhavati sa vāyupūto bhavati sa sūryapūto bhavati sa somapūto bhavati sa satyapūto bhavati sa sarvairdevairjñāto bhavati sa sarvairdevairanudhyāto bhavati sa sarveṣu tīrtheṣu snāto bhavati tena sarvaiḥ kratubhiriṣṭaṁ bhavati gāyatryāḥ ṣaṣṭisahasrāṇi japtāni bhavanti itihāsapurāṇānāṁ rudrāṇāṁ śatasahasrāṇi japtāni bhavanti | praṇavānāmayutaṁ japtaṁ bhavati | sa cakṣuṣaḥ paṅktiṁ punāti | ā saptamātpuruṣayugānpunātītyāha bhagavānatharvaśiraḥ sakṛjjaptvaiva śuciḥ sa pūtaḥ karmaṇyo bhavati | dvitīyaṁ japtvā gaṇādhipatyamavāpnoti | tṛtīyaṁ japtvaivamevānupraviśatyoṁ satyamoṁ satyamoṁ satyam || **7** ||

ityatharvaśiropaniṣatsamāptā

# APPENDIX

## Structure of the *Śruti* and of the *Smṛti*

## *Śruti* or *Veda*

The *Śruti* (audition) constitutes the revealed Tradition, of a 'non-human' order, and encompasses the four *Vedas*: *Ṛg*, *Yajus*, *Sāma* and *Atharva*. The term *veda*, from the root *vid*, to see/know, means traditional Wisdom, sacred Science. It represents the Knowledge which originates from the Principle and which, being of a synthetic order, can be comprehended not by way of the analytical or discursive mind (*manas*), as it belongs to empirical science, but by way of the supra-sensible faculty of the *buddhi*, or supra-conscious intuition (the *Noûs* of the ancient Greek philosophers).

The *Vedas* have originally been transmitted orally by Teacher to disciple, with great care; once put in writing, they were preserved in the original version, without any alterations. Therefore, the *Vedas* that we received contain, without any doubt, the exact words and ideas of the ancient Vedic Aryans. The *Vedas* encompass four major Sections: *Mantras* or *Saṁhitā*, *Brāhmaṇas*, *Āraṇyakas* and *Upaniṣads*.

The Aryans codified the *Vedas* in conformity with the four states of consciousness of life (*āśramas*). The student (*brahmacārin*) dedicated himself to the study of the *Saṁhitās*; the head of the household (*gṛhastha*) followed the injunctions of the *Brāhamaṇas*; the anchorite (*vānaprastha*) practiced contemplation according to the *Āraṇyakas*; the renunciate (*saṁnyāsin*) was guided by the wisdom of the *Upaniṣads*.

Another subdivision relates to the material dealt with; therefore every *Veda* contains three Sections: *Karmakāṇḍa*, *Upāsanakāṇḍa* and *Jñānakāṇḍa*. We therefore have the following correlations:

| | | |
|---|---|---|
| *Karmakāṇḍa* | *Mantras* or *Saṁhitās* | *Brahmacarya* |
| | *Brāhmaṇas* | *Gṛhasthya* |
| *Upāsanakāṇda* | *Āraṇyakas* | *Vānaprasthya* |
| *Jñānakāṇḍa* | *Upaniṣads* | *Saṁnyāsa* |

The *Karmakāṇḍa* section has to do with Rites and the performance of sacrifices, and it encompasses:

– *Mantras* or collections (*Saṁhitās*) of Hymns (*Mantras*) used in sacrifices.

– *Brāhmaṇas*. The *Brāhmaṇas* contain the rules for the performance of the sacrifices and also reveal the meaning of the *Mantras* that would be otherwise unknown. Both the *Brāhmaṇas* and the *Mantras* were indispensable for the sacrificial action (*karman*).

The *Upāsanakāṇḍa* section is constituted by the *Āraṇyakas* or 'Treatises of the forest.' These compositions were destined to those who had withdrawn into the *āśrams* of the forest in accordance with the third stage of life. They prescribe symbolic worship and describe various meditations to be carried out as a substitute for an actual sacrifice. They are texts of transition that mark the passage from the ritualism of the *Brāhmaṇas* to the Knowledge of the *Upaniṣads*.

The *Jñānakāṇḍa* section is constituted by the *Upaniṣads*, which are also called *Vedānta*, and which represents the final part of the Vedic texts. The teaching contained therein is the ultimate goal of the entire traditional knowledge. The very name *Upaniṣad* indicates that they destroy ignorance, and that they offer the opportunity to realize the supreme Knowledge (*paravidyā*). The term *Vedānta*, composed of the word *Veda* and the suffix *anta* (end, in the double meaning of conclusion and goal), indicates therefore both the concluding part of the *Vedas* and what is their ultimate goal: that is, Knowledge of *Brahman*.

Here is a table with the major *Upaniṣads* and the *Veda* to which they belong:

| *Vedas* | *Upaniṣads* |
|---|---|
| *Ṛg Veda* | *Aitareya, Kauṣītakī* |
| *Sāma Veda* | *Chāndogya, Kena* |
| *Yajur Veda* white *(śukla)* | *Bṛhadāraṇyaka, Īśa* |
| *Yajur Veda* black *(kṛṣṇa)* | *Taittirīya, Śvetāśvatara, Kaṭha, Maitry* |
| *Atharva Veda* | *Māṇḍūkya, Praśna, Muṇḍaka* |

## *Smṛti*

The *Smṛti* or 'memory' (remembered tradition) corresponds to transmitted knowledge and derives its authority from the *Śruti*. With the term *Smṛti* all the other texts that are not the *Vedas* are indicated. It encompasses:

1) *Darśana*. 'Point of view' or 'visual angle.' The *darśanas* are the different philosophical points of view from which a doctrine can be examined.[1] They are six:

– *Nyāya* or Logic. It examines the legitimate means to arrive at the knowledge of things. It has as its particular object the deductive or inferential argumentation (syllogism) and has developed techniques of debate (dialectic) whose goal is that of arriving at the right knowledge. Its codifier was Gautama and its main text is the *Nyāya Sūtra*.

– *Vaiśeṣika*, or distinctive knowledge, is a realistic atomistic pluralism. It concerns the knowledge of things as they are in themselves and proceeds to their classification. Its codifier was Kanada and its main text is the *Vaiśeṣika Sūtra*.

---

[1] Cf. Volume II of *Indian Philosophy*, by S. Radhakrishnan.

These first two *darśanas* have as their sphere of inquiry the analytical and distinctive aspects of the manifest nature. However they are not materialists as they propound the knowledge of the *ātman* as the ultimate goal.

– *Sāṁkhya* or 'enumeration', can also be considered as a dualistic realism. This *darśana* is also connected to the sphere of nature but considers the universal manifestation in terms of those Principles that determine its production. It moves from the universal to arrive at the particular. It enumerates twenty-five principles or *tattvas* out of which there are two principles of manifestation that are co-eternal, two poles, *puruṣa* and *prakṛti*, or Essence and Substance, in which manifestation takes place. Its codifier was Kapila and its main text is the *Sāṁkhyapravacana Sūtra*.

– *Yoga*, or union, adopts the philosophical and metaphysical presupposition of the *Sāṁkhya* but goes beyond the fundamental polarity of *puruṣa* and *prakṛti* which is re-integrated into the *Īśvara* principle. This *darśana* seeks to attain the spiritual realization or liberation through the practice of the eight means (*aṅgas*). Its codifier was Patañjali and its main text is the *Yoga Sūtra*.[1]

– *Pūrva Mīmāṁsā* or *Karma Mīmāṁsā* is the *darśana* of rituals. It offers an in-depth study of the *Vedas* in order to determine their true meaning, the precise sense of the *Śruti*, and to draw its implicit consequences in both the sphere of ritual sacrifice and in the practical one. Its codifier was Jaimini and its main text is the *Mīmāṁsā Sūtra*.

[1] Cf. Patañjali, *The Regal Way to Realization* (*Yogadarśana*). Op. cit.

– *Uttara Mīmāṁsā* or *Vedānta* (end of the *Vedas*). This is the metaphysical doctrine par excellence. Its fundamental theme is the quest for the Absolute as the ultimate Reality. It is based on the Teaching contained in the *Upaniṣads* and it has given expression to three main Schools: *Advaita* (Non-dualism) of Śaṅkara[1],*Dvaita-advaita* (qualified Monism) of Rāmānuja, and *Dvaita* (Dualism) of Madhva. These schools belong to *Vedānta* because they are founded on the *Upaniṣads* and because they consider *Brahman* as the ultimate Reality.

2) *Vedāṅga*. The term *vedāṅga* (member of the *Vedas*) is applicable to some auxiliary sciences of the *Vedas*. The fundamental treatises that refer to these sciences occupy a pre-eminent position in the *Smṛti* due to their direct relationship with the *Vedas*. They are six:

– *Śikṣā* (phonetics), is the science of correct pronunciation and of the symbolic and ideographic value of the letters.

– *Chandas* (prosody), knowledge of the different meters in relation to the modalities of the cosmic order they must express; knowledge of rhythm and of its cosmic relationships.

– *Vyākaraṇa* (grammar).

– *Nirukta* (etymology), the explanation of the important or difficult terms which is also based on the symbolic value of the letters.

---

[1] For a further deepening of *advaita Vedānta*, see Śankara's works: *Vivekacūḍāmaṇi*, *Aparokṣanubhuti*, *Ātmabodha*, and *Dṛgdṛiśyaviveka*. Aurea Vidyā, New York.

– *Jyotiṣa*, encompassing traditional astronomy and astrology together.

– *Kalpa*, encompassing the rules in relation to the carrying out of sacrifices.

3) *Upaveda*. Types of secondary knowledge, yet founded on a rigorously traditional basis. They refer to the sphere of practical applications. They are four. They are in relation to the four *Vedas*, which are intended as their respective principles:

– *Āyur Veda*, medical science, referring to the *Atharva Veda*.

– *Dhanur Veda,* military science, referring to the *Yajur Veda.*

– *Gandharva Veda,* music, referring to the *Sāma Veda*.

– *Sthāpatya Veda*, mechanics and architecture, referring to the *Ṛg Veda*.

Since the most ancient times, the other sciences were also entered into in depth, with particular regard to arithmetic, algebra, and geometry, which are encompassed under the denomination of *Gaṇita*, and which had considerable developments.

4) *Purāṇa*. These are ancient tales of mythological content that deal with the creation of the universe, the cosmic cycles, etc. Specific tendencies towards *bhakti* predominate. The most important ones are dedicated to *Viṣṇu*, (*Viṣṇu Purāṇa*) and to *Śiva* (*Śiva Purāṇa*).

5) *Itihāsa*. Epic poems, in their sacred meaning. *Itihāsas* are the *Rāmāyana* and the *Mahābhārata* of which the *Bhagavadgītā* is part.

6) *Dharmaśāstra.* A treatise (*śāstra*) that contains the cosmic Law (*Dharma*) and its application or interpretation.

7) *Āgamaśāstra.* A treatise founded on the Scriptures that is qualified as an authoritative text for the interpretation of the *Śruti*.

# GLOSSARY

## Note

The words in the glossary, transliterated from Sanskrit, follow the standard English alphabetical order. For simplicity, both short and long vowels are presented under one letter, and the three sibilants (*ś*, *ṣ*, *s*) appear under the letter *s*.

Abbreviations: m = masculine noun, f = feminine noun, n = neuter noun, N = name or proper noun, adj. = adjective, adv. = adverb, pro. = pronoun; n/m, for example, although grammatically masculine, indicates a neuter concept.

*Abhyāsa* (m): Practice of a method or teaching, continuous repetition of an effort.

*Abhāva* (m): Non-existence, non-being. Opposite of *bhāva*.

*Ācārya* (m): Master, Spiritual Teacher, one who has comprehended the Teaching.

*Advaitavāda* (m): Metaphysical doctrine of Non-duality formulated by Gauḍapāda and Śaṅkara.

*Adharma* (m): Not in conformity with the *dharma*, that which violates the universal Order (*Ṛta*) or the Law (*dharma*).

*Adhibhūta* (a,n): First elements of nature.

*Adhidaiva* (n): Universal Spirit, the first among the *Devas*, *Hiraṇyagarbha*.

*Adhiyajña* (m): The Origin of Sacrifices.

*Adhyāsa* (m): Superimposition, substitution. For Śaṅkara: 'Appearance in a given place of something which is known from elsewhere, on the basis of imaginative projection'.

*Adhyātma* (n): The *paramātman* (supreme Self), *ātman* as Principle, or primordial *ātman*. The intimate *ātman* (Self) of all beings.

*Adhyātmavidyā* (f): The Knowledge of the first principles or of the universal or primordial *ātman* (Self). Supreme Knowledge.

*Adhyātmayoga* (m): Supreme *Yoga*.

*Adṛṣṭa* (a, n): The not seen, the invisible. Principle non-perceived and non-perceivable by any faculty.

*A-dvaita* (n): Non-duality, absence of duality. (a): Without-a-second.

*Advaita Vedānta* (m): The non-dual *Vedānta*, codified by Gauḍapāda and Śaṅkara. Metaphysical *darśana* (*perspective*) which transcends dualism (*dvaita*) as well as monism (*aikya*). See also *Vedānta – Advaita Vedānta*.

*Advaitin* (m): One who follows the *Advaitavāda*, one who has realized Non-duality.

*Āgāmi karma* (n): One of the three types of *karma*. It is the *karma* which will unfold in the future and which, like the *saṁcitakarma*, can be avoided. See *Karma*.

*Agni* (m): Fire, Vedic divinity of the Fire.

*Ahaṁ* (m): Personal pronoun 'I', notion of 'I' as individualized reflection of consciousness, proceeding from the *ātman* (Self) through the mediation of the incarnate reflection of consciousness (*jīva*). Prototype of the *ahaṁkara* or sense of ego.

*Ahaṁkāra* (m): Literally, what makes up the ego; or the sense of the empirical ego. It constitutes consciousness in the individual state.
- emergence of the ego;
- extinction of the ego.

*Ainsoph* (n): The Absolute according to the *Qabbālāh*.

*Ajāti* (f): Non-generation.

*Ajātivāda* (m): The doctrine of non-generation presented by Gauḍapāda in his *Kārikā* (verse commentary) to the *Māṇḍūkya Upaniṣad*.

*Ajñāna* (n): Ignorance of metaphysical order (*avidyā*).

*Ākāra* (m): That which takes a form. Personal aspect of the Divine.

*Ākāśa* (m, n): The space, the universal ether which pervades the entire universe. It is the first of the five elements (*bhūta*), its characteristic being *śabda* (sound). Ether as quintessence of the Elements: fire, water and so on.

*Akṣara* (n, a): Imperishable, indestructible. One of the aspects of *Brahman*.

*Ānanda* (m): Absolute beatitude, pure happiness, joy without objects. Condition that inheres to the awareness of the fullness of one's Being. One of the three inseparable and consubstantial aspects of *ātman* (Self): *sat*, *cit*, *ānanda*.

*Ānandamaya* (m): Made or constituted (*maya*) of *ānanda* (beatitude).

*Ānandamayakośa* (m): The sheath of beatitude. The innermost and subjective casing. The seat of the *jīva* in the deep sleep state. As it is determined as *kośa* (layer, sheath) it is already in the plane of limitations and therefore does not represent the *ānanda* of *Brahman*.

*Ānātman* or *anātma* (m): That which is not *ātman*. The non-Self or *ahaṁkāra*, the empirical ego.

*Anattā* (*pāli*, f): Negation of the substantiality of the I.

*Annamaya* (a): Made or constituted of (*maya*) food (*anna*).

*Annamayakośa* (m): The sheath of food. The outermost sheath of *ātman* (Self). Gross sheath. It corresponds to the gross physical vehicle, in fact made up of transformed and assimilated food.

*Antaḥkaraṇa* (n): The internal organ, the 'mind' in its full extension and various *vṛtti* (modifications) which includes: *buddhi* (intellect, intuitive perception or direct discernment), *ahaṁkāra* (sense of self), *citta* (projecting memory, deposit of subconscious tendencies and predisposition) and *manas* (empirical selective mind).

*Apara* (a): Inferior, lesser; non supreme, relative.

*Aśabda* (m): The without sound. Referred to the silent *Brahman*, *Nirguṇabrahma* (without attributes), therefore beyond word/sound.

*Asat* (n): Non-being; non-reality, that which is not nor it exists in absolute.

*Asparśa* (a, n): Without contact, without relation, without support, absolute.

*Asparśavāda* (m): The doctrine of 'without contact', of non-relation, expounded by Gauḍapāda in the *Māṇḍūkyakārikā*.

*Asparśayoga* (m): The *yoga* of without contact, the *yoga* of pure consciousness as the non mediated realization of *ātman* (Self).

*Asparśin* (m): One who has realized the *Asparśayoga*, also one who follows the *Asparśavāda*.

*Āśrama* (m): Hermitage, life stage. The four life stages in the traditional Hindu society are: *brahmacārya* (celibacy and study), *gṛhasthya* (social and family responsibility), *vānaprasthya* (hermit stage), *saṁnyāsa* (total renunciation). States of consciousness which determine the corresponding life stages.

*Asura* (m): Genii of lower order, spirits of darkness, assimilated to disharmony.

*Aśvattha* (m): The Sacred Tree, mystical symbol of Life.

*Ātmabodha* (m): Consciousness of *ātman*, knowledge of the Self, title of one of Śaṅkara's treatises (*prākāraṇa*) considered as fundamental for the knowledge of the *Advaita Vedānta*.

*Ātman* (n): Self, Spirit, pure Consciousness, ontological 'I'. *Ātman* is the absolute in us, completely outside of time/space/cause, and as such is identical to *Brahman*. Absolute in itself.

*Aum* (m): The sacred syllable *Om* (*oṁkāra*) in its constituent elements. It symbolizes the Absolute. See *Om*.

*Avasthātraya* (n): The three states: waking/gross (*Viraṭ*), dream/subtle (*Hiraṇyagarbha*), deep sleep/causal (*Īśvara*) on which the *Vedānta* leads its investigation/discernment (*viveka*) to attain to the ultimate Reality or Fourth (*Turīya*).

*Avasthātrayasākṣin* (m): Witness of the three states; *ātman* (Self), pure Consciousness without modifications.

*Avatāra* (n): Descent of the Divine, *embodiment* of a Principle.

*Avidyā* (f): Metaphysical ignorance, ignorance with regard to the ultimate Reality, the noumenon, or the nature of Being. It is the individualized aspect of the universal ignorance, or *māyā*.

*Avyakta* (n): The undifferentiated, unmanifested condition of the Principle, universal One, undifferentiated condition of *prakṛti*/substance before it manifests.

*Āvṛtiśakti* (f): Veiling power of *maya-avidyā*. Also know as *āvaraṇaśakti*.

*Bhakta* (m): Devout. One who follows the path of *bhakti* (devotion). Person full of love for the Divine.

*Bhakti* (f): Ardent devotion, love for the Divine. Participation in the divine Being to the attainment of perfect union with It. For *Śaṅkara, bhakti* is the constant search for one's real nature. We have *aparabhakti* (non-supreme *bhakti*) and *parabhakti* (supreme *bhakti*).

*Bhaktiyoga* (m): The *yoga* of devotion. The *sādhanā* rests on filling the emotional body with love so as to cause the breaking through the level of the ego, which is necessary to attain the union with the Beloved.

*Bhāva* (m): Birth, phenomenal existence.

*Bhūta* (n): The existent, constituting substance, primordial element. First elements of nature. The five sensible elements out of which all bodies are made: earth, water, fire, air, ether (*ākāśa*).

*Bodha* (m): Intuitive knowledge, knowledge in that consciousness.

*Brahmā* (m): One of the three aspects of the Hindu *Trimūrti* or the threefold form with which the qualified Being, *Brahman saguṇa* or *Īśvara*, manifests. It is the manifesting principle of the universe that corresponds to the creator aspect, in relation with the conservator (*Viṣṇu*) and the transforming one (*Śiva*).

*Brahmacārin* (m): Person living the celibate and student *āsrama* (stage of life).

*Brahmacarya* (n): The first of the four traditional *āsramas* (stages of life), that of *brahmacārin* (celibate and student).

*Brahman or Brahma* (n): Is the absolute Reality, the Absolute in itself. That (*Tat*), which is totally transcendent and unconditioned, always identical to itself. One-without-a-second.

*Brahman nirguṇa* or *Nirguṇabrahma* (n, m): Non-qualified Reality, free (*nir*) of *guṇa* (attributes), absolute. It is applied to the absolute *Brahman*. See also *Brahman*.

*Brahman saguṇa* or *Saguṇabrahma* (n, m): Qualified Being, with *guṇa* (attributes). First qualification of *Nirguṇabrahma*. See also *Īśvara*.

*Brāhmaṇa* (n): First of the four traditional social orders (*varṇa*), the sacerdotal order, that of the *Sacerdotes* (ministers in a traditional sense). Text of liturgical exegesis annexed to the *Vedas*.

*Brahmanirvāṇa* (n): *Brahmanic nirvāṇa* or *Liberation*.

*Bṛhadāraṇyaka Upaniṣad*: The *Upaniṣad* of the great *Āranyaka*, one of the oldest and most important Vedic *Upaniṣads*. It contains the *mahāvākya* (great aphorism) *'aham brahmāsmi*: I am *Brahman*'.

*Brahmasūtra* (n): The *sūtras* on the *Brahman*, whose codification is attributed to Bādarāyaṇa/Vyāsa, containing the fundamental principles of *Vedānta*. Toghether with the *Upaniṣads* and the *Bhagavadgītā* it constitutes the *prasthānatraya* or the Threefold Science onf *Vedānta*.

*Brahmavidyā* (f): Knowledge of the Absolute, synonymous with *Brahmajñāna*.

*Buddhi* (n): Superior intellect, discerning intelligence, pure reason, intuition of the universal.

*Buddhimayakośa* (m): See *Vijñānamayakośa*.

*Buddhiyoga* (m): See *Jñānayoga*.

*Caitanya* (n): Consciousness. Spirit. Absolute pure Intelligence.

*Cakra* (n): 'Wheel', 'center'. The various *cakras* represent determinations of the energy/awareness, or *śakti*. Each *cakra* is in close correspondence with specific physical, mental and vital functions.

*Cit* (n): Pure and Absolute Consciousness (*caitanya*), pure Awareness, pure Intelligence, pure Knowledge. *Cit* is beyond any cognitive, representative process, beyond the mental and even beyond pure intellection or intellectual intuition (*buddhi*); yet it gives life to the mind itself, it provides support to its modifications and its functioning. One of the three inseparable and consubstantial aspects of *ātman* (Self): *sat*, *cit*, *ānanda*.

*Citta* (n): Mental substance through which *cit* condenses. Instrument of the mind through which the *jīva* materializes its individual world by giving form to the ideas and by making associations between them. One of the four faculties of the *antaḥkaraṇa* (internal organ), besides *buddhi*, *manas* and *ahaṁkāra*. Also contains memory impressions (*vāsanā*) and tendencies or mental seeds (*saṁskāra*).

*Daiva* (a): Sattvic condition of harmony/rythm.

*Dama* (m): Self-control; control of the mind; control of the various organs and body sensations.

*Dāna* (n): Donation, act of charity, generosity.

*Darśana* (n): Occasion in which to contemplate a Sage. Perspective, the term is used in relation to the doctrine of the *Vedas* and to the six orthodox school of Hindu traditional philosophy, which are: *Sāṁkhya*, *Yoga*, *Vaiśeṣika*, *Nyāya*, *Pūrva Mīmānsā* and *Uttara Mīmānsā* or *Vedānta*.

*Deva* (m): One who is resplendent, angelic being, Deity. It is also a title which comes at the end of the name of the great saints.

*Devayāṇa* (n): Path of Light, the way (*yāṇa*) of the Gods.

*Dhāraṇā* (f): Concentration, sixth means of the *Rajayoga* of Patañjali.

*Dharma* (m): Stems from the root *dhr*, which indicates supporting, preserving, wearing in general terms it designates a way of being, i.e. the essential nature of a being. Therefore, conformity with the Principle in accordance with the Universal Law of Equilibrium/Harmony (*Ṛta*). In metaphysical terms, that through which Harmony manifests as expression of the Unity of Being. In the individual order, it relates to the action which one will be able to perform in accordance with the Principle (*karma-dharma*), to attain liberation. Fundamental *dharma* of each human being is to become aware of and to realize in practice one's own divine Nature, which permeates all beings.

*Dharmakṣetra* (m): Field of the *dharma*. See also *kurukṣetra*.

*Dhyāna* (n): Yogic meditation; costant and continuous flow of awareness on a seed of meditation. Seventh means of *Rājayoga* of *Patañjali*.

*Dhyānayoga* (m): *Yoga* of meditation.

*Dṛgdṛśyaviveka* (m): Discernment between *ātman* (the spectator) and non-*ātman* (the spectacle). Title of a work, fundamental for the comprehension of the *Advaita Vedānta*, attributed to Śaṅkara.

*Dṛk* (m): the seer, the spectator, one who sees, who perceives (*draṣṭṛ*).

*Dṛśya* (f): the visible, the object of vision or knowledge. The spectacle of which the *ātman* is the spectator or witness.

*Dvaita* (n, a): Duality, dualism; dualistic school; dual.

*Dvija* (m): Twice born, born anew to the immortality of the *ātman*.

*Gauḍapāda*: Master of the *Advaita Vedānta* of which he was the first codifier. Śaṅkara's spiritual Master. Author of the *Māṇḍūkyakārikā* (or *Gauḍapādayakārikā*), verse commentary to the *Māṇḍūkya Upaniṣad*, where the *Ajātivāda* (doctrine of the non-generation, non-creation) and the *Asparśayoga* (*yoga* of no support) are exposed.

*Gṛhastha* (m): The second of the traditional *āśramas* (stages of life). One who lives the state of head of family; the state of who fulfills his responsibilities.

*Guṇa* (m): Thread, rope, constituent quality, (pl).: principial attributes/qualities of *prakṛti*/substance or qualitative principles of the universal substance (*prakṛti*) which are at the base of manifestation. The three *guṇas* of the *Sāṁkhya darśana* are: *sattva*, *rajas* and *tamas*.

*Guru* (m): Instructor, spiritual Teacher (*ācārya*), one who removes (*ru* stands for removing) ignorance (*gu* stands for obscurity or ignorance). Instructor in the *Vedas*, who performs purifying ceremonies.

*Haṭhayoga* (m): *Yoga* of the physiological well-being. Aims at perfection and dominion of the body, for its transformation into the Temple of the Spirit.

*Hiraṇyagarbha* (m): Golden germ, cosmic egg *(brahmāṇḍa)*. The second of the three states of Being. The totality of the subtle universal manifestation, which comprehends its individual corresponding subtle aspect (*taijasa*).

*Indriya* (n): Literally, power; indicates both the faculty of the senses and their corporeal organs. Together they constitute an instrument of knowledge (*jñānendriya*) and action (*karmendriya*). The internal modification of the mind associated with the sensory organ itself.

*Īśvara* (m): Divine Person, it represents what we could define as the personified God. It is the first determination of the absolute *Brahman*, and it comprehends the entire field of manifestation: gross, subtle and causal, both from the cosmic and individual points of view. God-person and Universal *Puruṣa*.

*Jāgrat* (n): Waking state. The other ones are: *svapna* or dream state, *suṣupti* dreamless sleep state and *Turīya*, which transcends them all.

*Jijñāsā* (f): Research.

*Jīva* (m): Living being (*jīvin*), individuated Soul, reflection of consciousness of the *ātman* on the universal plane. It produces movement and activity within itself and engenders, through *ahaṁkāra*, the subject (self/*aham)* as well as the object (world/*idam)* of experience or knowledge.

*Jīvanmukta* (pp): Liberated during life, one who has extinguished the threefold Fire.

*Jīvātman* (m): The *ātman* as reflected in the *jīva*, Soul.

*Jñāna* (n): Knowledge, from *jñā* (to know), is identical to the Greek gnosis. Cathartic, liberating knowledge. Also one of the qualities of the Lord (*Bhagavad*): wisdom, intelligence.

*Jñānacakṣus* (n): Eye of vision or knowledge.

*Jñānakāṇḍa* (n): Section of the *Vedas* that regards Knowledge.

*Jñānayoga* (m): The *yoga* of Knowledge. Its postulates are: intuitive discernment (*viveka*) between the real (*ātman*, Self) and the non-real (empirical self, non-Self, i.e., *ahaṁkāra*, *an-ātman*), detachment (*vairāgya*) and, reintegration into the Absolute through Knowledge/awareness.

*Jñānendriya* (n): Organ of perception: the five senses. The five faculties of sensation.

*Jñāni* (m): Knower, one who practices the *Jñānayoga*, realized being.

*Kaivalya* (n): State of isolated Unity, isolation from the threefold world. It is the supreme absoluteness of *Brahman nirguṇa*, state of Consciousness devoid of duality realized by the pure *jñānin*.

*Kāma* (m): Desire, coveting, greed, attachment to the sensory world.

*Kāma-manas* (n): Mental condition of complete conformity with desire; relationship between desire and empirical mind; emotion that proceeds from imagination. It is the characteristic of *mano-mayakosa*.

*Karma* or *Karman* (n): Action, activity, principle of causality, effects resulting from an action. Also rite. It is the inertia of the mental mass of the subject which pushes it to act, think, identify and be in a specific condition. It can be considered both as cause and as effect of the action, which forces the being into *saṁsāra*, (perennial becoming).

- initiatory action and its premises
- egoistic action
- fruit of action

- right action
- the five principles/causes of action
- inexorable necessity of action
- *karma/dharma*
- renouncing the fruits of action
- transcendence of action.

*Karmakāṇḍa* (n): Section of the *Vedas* dealing with ritual action.

*Karmayoga* (m): *Yoga* of action.

*Karmendriya* (n): Five organs of action: voice (*vāc*), hands (*pāṇi*), feet (*pāda*), generative organs (*upasthā*) excretion organs (*pi*).

*Kartā* (n): agent, acting subject.

*Kośa* (m): Shell, envelope, sheath, energetic sheath. According to *Vedānta* five sheaths envelop the Self or *ātman*: *ānandamayakośa*, *vijñānamayakośa*, *manomayakośa*, *prāṇomayakośa* and *annamayakośa*.

*Kṣatriya* (m): One who belongs to the regal/military order, to the order of the judges and the politicians, one who supports law and justice; one of the four traditional social orders (*varṇa*); it corresponds to the guardians of Plato's Politèia.

*Kṣetra* and *kṣetrajña* (n, m): The field and knower of the field.

*Kuṇḍalinī* (f): Literally, the rolled up. Serpentine force; nervous and psychical force placed in the lotus at the base of the spine (*mūlādhāracakra*).

*Kurukṣetra* (n): 'Battle field'. Also *tapahkṣetra*.

*Laya* (m): Dissolution/transformation, destruction, absorption. See *Pralaya*.

*Liṅga* (n): Subtle character, reason. Phallus as symbol of energy. Its elliptic form with its two poles represents the Diad, the bipolarity expressed in creation.

*Loka* (m): World. Cosmos, not to be viewed in a strictly spatial sense. Condition of existence as determined by the state of consciousness/knowledge.

*Mahat* (n): The Great; cosmic Intelligence; the great Mind. Principle of the cosmic manifestation according to the *Sāṁkhya darśana*. First effect of *mūlaprakṛti*.

*Maṭha* or *Maṭh* (m): sacred place, monastery, cenoby.

*Mahāvākya* (m): Great aphorism; the Vedic great aphorisms in which the *Vedānta* Doctrine is synthesized. The main *mahāvākyas* are four: *ahaṁ brahmāsmi*, I am *Brahman* (*Bṛhadāraṇyaka Upaniṣad*: I.IV.10; in the 'black' *Yajur Veda*); *Tat tvam asi*, That thou art (*Chāndogya Upaniṣad*: VI.VII.7; in the *Sama Veda*); *Prajñānaṁ Brahma*, *Brahman* is pure consciousness (*Aitareya Upaniṣad*: V.3; in the *Ṛg Veda*); *Ayam ātmā brahma*, This *ātman* is *Brahman* (*Māṇḍūkya Upaniṣad*: II; in the *Atharva Veda*). The *mahāvākya* must be meditated upon in the light of supraconscious intuition (*buddhi*) and not be object of rational analysis of the empirical mind (*manas*).

*Manana* (n): reflection.

*Manas* (n): Mind, internal sense, individuated empirical mind, conscience endowed of rational/analytical ability, imaginative mind.

*Māṇḍūkyakārikā* (f): Verse Commentary (*kārikā*) of Gauḍapāda to the *Māṇḍūkya Upaniṣad*. Traditionally this work is considered *Āgamaśāstra* (Authoritative Treatise on the Scriptures), and has, in its turn, been commented by *Śaṅkara*. In the *Māṇḍūkyakārikā*: Gauḍapāda and Śaṅkara expound the *Asparśayoga*, the *yoga* of without support or relation.

*Manomayakośa* (m): The sheath constituted by the empirical mind, selective/instinctual mind that operates through attraction/ repulsion. In it, is active the sense of ego (*ahaṁkāra*).

*Mantra* (m): Section of the *Vedas*, power words or sounds, hymns used in ritual acts, sacred word, formulae or verses expressed or meditated upon during concentration and meditation, vibrating thought.

*Manvantara* (m): Period of *Manu*, cosmic cycle that comprehends four *yugas*: *satya*, *tretā*, *dvāpara* and *kali*.

*Mātrā* (f): Measure; metric quantity; length of each foot (*pāda*), in the sense of paragraph, division, part.

*Maya* (a): particle meaning made of, constituted by.

*Māyā* (f): Metaphysical ignorance, the world of names and forms as vital phenomenon; all that is modification superimposed (*upādhi*) on the pure Consciousness of the Self, *ātman*; conformed movement, *Īśvara*'s 'sleep dream'.

*Moha* (m): Bewilderment, confusion, blinding.

*Mokṣa* (m): Liberation, the attainment of eternal Beatitude as outcome of the recognition of the ultimate Truth; deliverance from ignorance (*avidyā*) from relativity/becoming and from all that constitutes *māyā* as the superimposed modification on the pure Consciousness of the *ātman*; the last of the four *puruṣārthas* (ends of a being. See *vidyā*).

*Mukta* (pp): Liberated, Awakened, Realized being.

*Mūlādhāracakra* (n): One of the seven *cakra* at the base of the spinal column where *kuṇḍalinī* is rolled.

*Mumukṣutā* or *mumukṣutva* (n, f): Intense aspiration for delivery from all bondage; longing for liberation as result of maturity of consciousness. In the *Vedānta* path, it is one of the four necessary means to penetrate the world of causes and break the chain of the superimpositions that veil Reality.

*Muni* (m): Ascetic person practising silence. One who knows the value of silence (*mauna*). State of consciousness of one who has realized the non-qualified Absolute.

*Naiṣkarmya* (n): State of one who has transcended both *dharma* and *adharma*.

*Nāman* (n): Name; complementary to *rūpa*, form. According to *Vedānta*, that which has a name and also a form and vice versa. The dyad *nāmarūpa* makes the differentiated and individuated being emerge from the substratum of unqualified Being. As Śaṅkara states, *nāma-rūpa* are mere mental modifications.

*Nāmarūpa* (n): 'Name/form'. The world of names and forms that constitute becoming; constitutive elements; elements that constitute and characterize individuality. See *nāma*.

*Neti neti*: 'not this, not this'. Aphorism of negation through which the *jñānayogin* successively discards all that which is appearance, relative and transitory, and through discernment (*viveka*) and detachment (*vairāgya*) attains *Brahman*, the permanent and absolute Substratum.

*Nirākāra* (n): Impersonal aspect of the Divine.

*Nirguṇa* (a): Free from *guṇa*, non-qualified, absolute, it is applied to *Brahman*.

*Nirguṇabrahma* (n, m): See *Brahman nirguṇa*.

*Nirvāṇa* (n): Extinction, solution. Also *nivṛtti*. Supreme state in which the *jīva* has resolved into the non dual *ātman*.

*Nirvikalpa* (a): Free from differentiation, immutable, absolute, transcendent. It refers to *Brahman* Consciousness, non-dual, eternal and unchanging.

*Nirvikalpasamādhi* (m): *Samādhi* free from differentiations. Consciousness totally free from differentiations and, therefore, from duality. It represents the integral merging into the One-without-a-second.

*Niyama* (m): Observances. The second step or means (*aṅga*) of the *Rājayoga* of Patañjali. The observances are: purity, contentment, burning aspiration, study, and abandon to the Lord.

*Nyāya* (n): One of the six *darśanas*, codified by Gautama. The specific meaning of the word *nyāya* is: logic or method.

*Non-ātman* (m): See *anātman*.

*Om*: The sacred syllable among all. Symbol of the Absolute, of *Brahman* and also of all the concepts the human being has of the Supreme, the Divine. This syllable is part of almost all *mantras*. The symbol itself is the symbol of Totality and of absolute Unity (non-duality) and is regarded as sacred in all of India. The syllable *Om* (*oṁkāra*) is seed of meditation, as well as its parts: *A*, *U*, *M*, which express the gross, subtle and causal planes respectively. *Om* with sound, represents the qualified Being, *Brahman Saguṇa*, while the silent *Om* represents the non qualified Being or *Brahman nirguṇa*.

*Om Tat Sat*: '*Om*, That is the Reality' is also considered a *mahāvākya*, which is in the 'black' *Yajur Veda*.

*Pāda* (m, n): Foot, in the sense of paragraph; division, part. Measure, in rhythmical poetry.

*Para* (a): Other, different; superior, supreme.

*Paramātman* (n): the Supreme *ātman* (Self) which is identical to *Brahman*; supreme Spirit. See *Puruṣottama*.

*Paravidyā* (f): Supreme Knowledge, science of the Greater Mysteries, metaphysical Knowledge.

*Patañjali*: Codifier of the *Yoga darśana* (*Rājayoga* or Regal *yoga*).

*Pitś* (n): Mani, spirits of the ancestors.

*Pitśyāṇa* (n): Way of the ancestors (*Mani*).

*Pradhāna* (n): Primeval element or 'nature', is equivalent to *prakṛti*.

*Prājña* (m): Causal body of the human *jīva*. In *prājña* multiplicity and duality are reintegrated into unity of undifferentiated consciousness, as synthesis of knowledge. It also represents the *jīva* in the deep sleep state (*suṣupti*). Third state in Gauḍapāda's doctrine (see *Māṇḍūkyakārikā*), represents in the individual order, what *Īśvara* is in the Universal order.

*Prakṛti* (f): nature, universal substance, *natura naturans*, the substance by which all sensible and intelligible forms are made. For *Vedānta*, it is the equivalent of *māyā*, *pradhāna* or *avyakta*.

*Pralaya* (m): Dissolution; return into undifferentiated state; dissolution of the manifestation, at the end of a 'day' of *Brahmā* (*kalpa*).

*Prāṇa* (m): Vital breath, cosmic breath, vital energy. Totality of the universal energies, therefore it exists on all levels of manifestation. It is noumenal movement. Original vital energy.

*Prāṇamayakośa* (m): Sheath of the vital energy. It is constituted by the subtle energies that keep the gross body alive and active.

*Praṇava* (m): That which is pronounced. The sacred syllable *Om*. See *Om*.

*Prāṇāyāma* (m): Prāṇic breathing, control of the *prāṇa*. *Yoga* breathing practice. The fourth means of Patañjali's *Yogadarśana*.

*Prārabdhakarma* (n): Result or effect of past actions which have reached maturation (*prārabdha*), which cannot, therefore, be neutralized, unlike the *sāmcitakarma* and the *āgāminkarma*.

*Prasthānatraya* (n): Threefold Testimony. The Threefold Science of *Vedānta* constituted by the classical *Upaniṣads*, the *Brahmasūtra* and the *Bhagavadgītā*.

*Pratyāhāra* (m): Abstraction, withdrawal from the sensory activities. Fifth means in Patañjali's *Yogadarśana*. Leads to introspection, i.e. the mind detaches from the influence of the external impressions and turns into itself.

*Puruṣa* (m): Positive principle whose presence stimulates *prakṛti*'s activity. For the *Sāṁkhya darśana*, it is the spirit which united with *prakṛti* manifests the world. Spiritual Principle of the human being. See also *Īśvara*.

*Puruṣottama* (m): Supreme *Puruṣa*. Universal Spirit.

*Pūrva Mīmāṁsā* (f): Anterior *Mīmāṁsā*, also called *Karma Mīmāṁsā* or *Dharma Mīmāṁsā* in that it relates to the sphere of action and ritual action. One of the six *darśanas*, was codified by Jaimini.

*Qabbālāh*: Reception, transmission, represents the esoteric part of the Old Testament.

*Rāga/dveṣa* (m, n): Attachment/aversion, attraction/repulsion caused by sensory objects.

*Rajas* (n): One of the three *guṇa* (the other two being *tamas* and *sattva*) which corresponds to activity, energy, desire, fire, passion and responds to expansion, dynamic movement and development. In the hierarchical order of manifestation *rajas* corresponds to the subtle plane, *tamas* to the gross and *sattva* to the causal plane.

*Rājayoga (m)*: Regal *yoga*. *Yoga darśana*, codified by Patañjali.

*Ṛṣi* (n): Seer. The great Sages who heard the *Śruti* (Tradition) and handed it down through the *Vedas* and the *Upaniṣads*. The expression, 'The *Ṛṣi* said', is tantamount as to saying 'So it is said in the Sacred Texts'.

*Ṛta* (n): Universal Order/harmony.

*Rūpa* (n): Form, look, character; nature, character, peculiarity; color, exterior perceivable appearance; forms through which life manifests. One of the five *tanmātra* or sensible qualities: the color/form which is characteristic of the *tejas* (fire) element. See *nāma* and *nāmarūpa*.

*Śabda* (m): Sound, verbal testimony, qualified aspect of *Brahman* in its sound *Om*, one of the five *tanmātra*.

*Sādhanā* (f): Name given to any discipline which is ardently followed with perseverance in order to progress in the spiritual life, spiritual effort undergone for realization by the disciple.

*Saguṇa* (a): With attributes, qualified; it refers to *Brahman* endowed with *guṇa* (attributes) or the qualified Being, first superimposition on *Nirguṇabrahma*. Equivalent to *Īśvara*.

*Saguṇabrahma* (n, m): See *Brahman saguṇa*.

*Śakti* (f): Energy, virtual power of *māyā*, energy of manifestation, dynamic energy induced by the presence of the positive immobile pole (*Śiva*), name of the divine mother as divine primordial energy.

*Sākṣin* (m): Witness, spectator that does not participate in and is detached from experiential events and empirical knowledge. It refers to the *ātman* as the Witness of the three states.

*Śama* (m): Mental calm; tranquility of the mind which has stopped adhering to the outer and inner objects; cessation of mental projections, extinction of thought movement. One of the qualities, part of the third qualification, of the *Advaita* disciple.

*Samādhāna* (n): Mental steadfastness. One of the six virtues or qualities, which together constitute the third qualification of the *Advaita* disciple. Condition of continuous concentration on *Brahman*.

*Samādhi* (m): Its etymology means transcendent identity, that which transcends the apparent formal distinction; state of union (*yoga*) with the personified Divine (*Īśvara*) and of identity (*aikya*) with the impersonal Divine (*Brahman*) attained by the *yogi*. *Samādhi* involves a series of stages which are described in several texts (e.g. *Dśgdśśyaviveka* and *Yogadarśana*).

*Samatā* (f): Equanimity.

*Saṁcita karma* (n): Delayed effect or result of past actions (*karma*) which has accumulated but not reached maturation and actualization, and which, in the present state of realization, can easily be destroyed.

*Saṁnyāsa* (m): Total renunciation, the last of the four traditional life stages (*āśrama*). State of consciousness in which the non-reality of the qualifications is recognized.

*Saṁnyāsin* (m): Renouncing ascetic. One who, having comprehended, has renounced everything.

*Saṁprasāda* (m): Constant and imperturbable serenity. *Pax Profunda.*

*Saṁsāra* (m): Perennial cycle of becoming; transmigrating within becoming as continual passage through different conditions of consciousness and therefore of existence; indefinite succession of birth/life/rebirth to which liberation (*mokṣa*) puts an end. It corresponds to the uninterrupted chain of cause/effect, for which *karma* ties the individual to becoming.

*Saṁskāra* (m): 1. Preparatory purification rites for consecration, clothing, etc., preparatory rites in general. 2. Causal seeds of action engendered by the tendencies that are present in the mental substance (*citta*) and deriving from experiences, actions, thoughts produced in the present existence as well as in the innumerable prior ones.

*Saṅga* (m): Attachment. See also *rāga/dveṣa*.

*Śaṅkara*: 1. Codifier of the *Advaita Vedānta*, metaphysical *darśana* which transcends the religious dualism and ontological monism itself. He lived between 788 and 820 a.d. Compiled important commentaries (*bhāṣya*) to numerous *Upaniṣads*, to the *Brahmasūtra*, the *Bhagavadgītā*, and other works in which he summarizes the teaching and the practice through which to attain *Advaita* realization. Śaṅkara was a disciple of Govindapāda who in turn was a disciple of Gauḍapāda. He established himself as a strenuous defender of the *Sanātanadharma*, the Doctrine of the pure Vedic Tradition, and instituted ten monastic orders to prevent degeneration of spiritual practice. Through the codifying of the *Advaita*, he provided a solid ontological and metaphysical base for all the cults of the time. He founded four monasteries/*maṭha* at the four cardinal points of India, focal points of the very powerful influence still perceived today. 2. (m): One who donates every sort of good, name of *Śiva* that means: auspicious, propitious, benevolent, giver of joy and prosperity. *Śiva* is *Śaṅkara*, one who with his Grace causes *saṁ*, or *ānanda* at the highest level.

*Śānta* (m): Totally pacified, perfectly quiet.

*Śāntānām* (m): Mental calm. See *śama* and *śānta*.

*Śāstra* (n): Code, teaching, sacred text. It indicates all sacred Scriptures in general.

*Sat* (n): Being, pure Being. Absolute and pure existence, contrary to *asat*: that which has no existence. *Sat*, *cit*, *ānanda* are the three consubstantial aspects of Being.

*Sat-cit-ānanda* (n): Absolute Existence (*sat*), Consciousness (*cit*) and Beatitude (*ānanda*). The three consubstantial aspects of *Brahman* and therefore of *ātman*.

*Sattva* (n): Being, existence in itself, essence, wisdom, intellectual light, one of the three *guṇa* (the other two being *rajas* and *tamas*), which corresponds to equilibrium, harmony, light, purity. In the hierarchical order of manifestation *sattva* corresponds to the causal plane, *rajas* to the subtle and *tamas* to the gross plane.

*Savikalpa* (a): With differentiation, that which contains in itself differentiation, differentiated, formal.

*Savikalpa samādhi* (m): Transcendental contemplation in which the distinction of subject and object is still latent. It leads to the realization of *Brahman Saguṇa*.

*Sephiroth*: Numeration, according to the *Qabbālāh* they are the Gods creators of the universe, the Principles that activate the emergence of manifestation. Hierarchical powers that operate in the universal and infra-individual planes.

*Siddha* (m): Perfect in *yoga*, one who has realized *yogi*c perfection.

*Siddhi* (f): Fulfillment, *yogi*c perfection; psychical powers obtained through *yoga* practice.

*Śiva* (m): Beneficial, propitious, one of the three aspects of the *Trimūrti*. The Divine when considered in its transforming and resolving aspect (*mūrti*), but when in union with its *śakti* (*Pārvatī*) it takes the function of creator; as such it is symbolized by the *liṅga*. Śaivism separates the aspect of creating from those of conserving and dissolving, so that the aspects that *Śiva* takes, and those of the corresponding *śakti*, are differentiated, but at the same time, *Śiva* is considered as the sole and absolute Principle. For *Vedānta*, *Śiva* is the always and everywhere present, One-without-a-second, i.e. *Brahman*.

*Smṛti* (f): Texts of the remembered, indirect or mediated Tradition. Works by human memory and not of direct spiritual inspiration or illumination.

*Sparśa* (m): Contact, relation.

*Śraddhā* (n): Faith. Confident adherence to the truth expounded in the Scriptures and by the *guru*. One of the six virtues or qualities, which together constitute the third qualification of the *Advaita* disciple.

*Śruti* (f): Audition, the Tradition of the Heard, sacred Knowledge which was immediately revealed (*Veda*), that which was heard by the ancient Seers (*Ṛṣi*) as divine Sounds. One of the names given the *Vedas*. The *Śruti* is constituted by the *Vedas*. For a Traditional comprehension of the of the *Bhagavadgītā*, see the Preface.

*Śūdra* (m): One of the four traditional social orders (*varṇa*), it is equivalent of worker. One who lays the foundations of human wellbeing with service activities.

*Suṣupti* (f): State of deep sleep. Sleep without dream, corresponds to the causal body/plane.

*Sūtra* (n): Thread, rope; aphorism, verse. Text that codifies the fundamental principles of the various philosophical *darśanas*. Metaphorically also the *ātman* that connects all existential planes.

*Sūtrātma* (n): Thread of *ātman* (Self); word that equates to *Hiraṇyagarbha*, subtle universal aspect which comprises the different individualities. Continuity of consciousness of the *ātman*.

*Svadharma* (m): *Dharma* inherent to the proper nature of a being.

*Svapna* (n): Dream, dream state.

*Taijasa* (m): The luminous, from *tejas* (fire); the second quarter, *pāda* (foot) of the *ātman*. It constitutes the subtle plane of formal manifest existence and therefore the threefold subtle body (*sūkṣmaśarīra*). It corresponds to *Hiraṇyagarbha* in the universal order.

*Tanmātra* (m): Literally, the measure of this; extension or boundary of something. It indicates the substantial quality of an object, but more specifically of the elements that are forming it; also what makes the experience possible through the specific and corresponding sensory organs of knowledge (*jñānendriya*).

*Tamas* (n): One of the three *guṇa* (the other two being *rajas* and *sattva*), which corresponds to obscurity, inertia, passiveness, and to inert immobility, etc. It faces down, and since it represents the maximum condensation of the potentiality of the being, it corresponds to ignorance (*avidyā*). In the hierarchical order of manifestation *tamas* corresponds to the gross plane, *rajas* to the subtle and *sattva* to the causal plane.

*Tao*: The Book of the Way, the Traditional Chinese Metaphysical Teaching, which toghether with the *Te*, The Book of the Virtue, forms the *Tao Te King*, the Sacred Treatise codified directly by Lao Tze.

*Tapas* (n): Heat, ascetic heat, austerity; ardent aspiration, one of the five *niyamas* of Patañjali's *Rājayoga*.

*Tat* (pr): That. In the *Upaniṣads* it indicates the unqualified Absolute, *Brahman* devoid of attributes or *Nirguṇabrahma*.

*Tattva* (n): Quiddity, truth, principle; category, elemental principle. The twenty five principles, categories in the *Sāṁkhya darśana*, and the twenty six ones of the *Yoga darśana*.

*Tejas* (n): Energy, light, *splendour*, brilliance, fire (inner).

*That* (pr): Term with which the Absolute is indicated. See *Tat*.

*Titikṣā* (n): Persevering patience coupled with the spiritual ideal. Moral courage. Tolerance garnished by sympathetic understanding. One of the six virtues or qualities, which together constitute the third qualification of the *Advaita* disciple.

*Trimūrti* (f): Threefold manifestation, *Brahmā*, *Viṣṇu*, *Śiva*.

*Turīya* (a, n): The Fourth, Fourth state (*Caturtha*), which is real/ absolute and constitutes the necessary non-dual substratum of all relative states with their contents. *Turīya* is *Nirguṇabrahma* and represents the Absolute, the Infinite and the metaphysical Zero. It can be described only by negations: Unborn, Non-caused, Non-limited, Non-conditioned, Non-determined. It is One-without-a-second (*advaita*) that comprehends and transcends all duality and even the Principle or ontological unity itself (*Īśvara*).

*Upādhi* (m): Superimposition, that which is superimposed on the Self, *ātman*, thereby constituting at the same time both a vehicle and a conditioning.

*Upaniṣad* (n): Hindu Sacred Texts, also called *Vedānta*, which are grouped in Ancient, Intermediate and Recent *Upaniṣads*, and also in Major and Minor *Upaniṣads*, and which are part of the *Śruti*. Etymologically the word *Upaniṣad* indicates the act of sitting next to someone, in reverential attitude, referring to the disciple at the feet of the Master receiving esoteric knowledge, secret wisdom. Also, sessions or esoteric Teachings. For Śaṅkara their purpose is to destroy ignorance/*avidyā*, by providing means apt to attain supreme Knowledge.

*Uparati* (n): Inwardly absorption. One of the six virtues or qualities, which together constitute the third qualification of the *Advaita* disciple.

*Uttara Mīmāṁsā* (f): Further *Mīmāṁsā*, also called *Brahma Mīmāṁsā*, is essentially and directly concerning *Brahmavidyā:* it constitutes *Vedānta* and has traditionally been attributed to Vyāsa.

*Vairāgya* (n): Detachment from every form of fruit of action, from all conditions and all objects of attachment; renunciation founded on personal reflection and on the teaching received from the *guru*.

*Vaiśeṣika* (n): One of the six *darśanas*, codified by Kaṇāda. This *darśana* is directed to the knowledge of individual things as such, considered in a distinctive manner in the contingent existence.

*Vaiśvānara* (m): Totality of existence at the gross state of manifestation. Gross totality (*Virāṭ*). On the universal plane, it corresponds to the individual gross/physical body (*viśva*). A first state of Being described in the *Māṇḍūkya Upaniṣad* as the Self, *ātman*, in the waking state.

*Vaiśya* (m): The third of the traditional social orders (*varṇa*), that of the producers of wealth.

*Vaitathya* (n): Non-real nature of that which is apparent and illusory.

*Vānaprasthya* (n): The third of the traditional stages of life (*āśrama*). State of one who, having done its duty as head of family, retires into a life of renunciation and meditation. It is a state of consciousness in which the withdrawal from the world is motivated by the *jīva*'s maturity and not by the escape from one's own duties.

*Varṇa* (m): Color, social order. The four traditional social orders: *brāhmaṇa* (*Sacerdotes*, ministers in a traditional semse), *kśatriya* (lawmakers or warriors), *vaiśya* (producers of wealth) and *śūdra* (workers). Also sound as essence of each letter.

*Vāsanā* (f): Subconscious mental impression induced by experience, action and thought, or arising out of indefinite epochs of the past through accumulated *karma*. Furrows in the mental substance (*citta*), they constitute the true seeds (*saṁskāra*) of thought, and also of rebirth.

*Veda* (m): Literally, what has been seen, realized by the Sages (*Ṛṣi*); supreme Knowledge, sacred Science. The four great collections: *Ṛg Veda*, *Sāma Veda*, *Yajur Veda* and *Atharva Veda*, contain the exposition of that sacred and traditional Science in its highest expressions, and form the *Śruti*.

*Vedānta* (m): End of the Vedas; is one of the six *darśanas*. Within *Vedānta* are three main currents:
– *Advaita Vedānta* (non-dualism) codified by Śaṅkarācārya.
– *Viśiṣṭādvaita* (mitigated O qualified monism) codified by Rāmānuja.
– *Dvaita Vedānta* (dualism) codified by Madhva.

*Vedānta – Advaita Vedānta* (m): Non-dual *Vedānta*; metaphysical *darśana* that transcends both dualism and monism;
– Constitution of the being according to *Advaita Vedānta*.

- With reference to the manifestation of life
- Subject and object according to *Advaita Vedānta*.

*Vidyā* (f): Knowledge of Reality; consciousness meditation that leads to realization, classified as lesser (*apara*) and greater (*para*). Regarding the *puruṣārthas* (ends of a being), the *aparavidyā* is in relation with the first three ends of the human being: *dharma* or rectitude, *ārtha* or well being, *kāma* or legitimate desire. The *paravidyā*, as expounded in the *Upaniṣads*, regards the ultimate end of the human being: *mokṣa* or liberation.

*Vijñāna* (n): Pure intellect, synonym with *buddhi*, as synthetic/integrating knowledge. Also Knowledge in the sense of awareness/consciousness.

*Vijñānamayakośa* or *buddhimayakośa* (m): Sheath made of intellect, envelope of superior intellect, or *buddhi*. Its nature is represented by intellective reason, intuitive discernment. When developed it balances *manomayakośa*, when made 'sattvic' it is able to contemplate universal archetypes.

*Vikṣepaśakti* (f): The projective power of *avidyā/māyā* through which, in place of the Real, the image of the universe of names and forms is projected. It is related to *āvṛtiśakti* (veiling power).

*Virāṭ* or *Virāj* (m): The totality of the gross manifestation (*vaiśvānara*).

*Viṣṇu*: Conserving aspect of the *Trimūrti*.

*Viśva* (n): All, as considered in its unity/entirety; consciousness in the waking state in which the individual *jīva* experiences gross objects.

*Viveka* (m): Intuitive discernment, discrimination between real and non-real, noumenon and phenomenon, which leads to detachment (*vairāgya*) from the non-real and to becoming conscious of Reality.

*Vivekacūḍāmaṇi* (f): The Great Jewel of Discernment, title of a work by *Śrī* Śaṅkarācārya which is a fundamental text for the realization of the *Advaita Vedānta*. In it, a dialogue takes place between a Master and a neophyte where all the principal aspects of the doctrine of Non-duality are thoroughly researched in a highly philosophical and poetical way, in both cognitive and operative aspects.

*Vyāsa*: According to Tradition, this name indicates, not a historical or legendary figure, but the collective entity that gave order and definitively established the traditional texts, such as the *Mahābhārata*, the eighteen *Purāṇa* the *Brahmasūtra* and the *Veda Saṁhitā*. It is a truly intellectual function, which could also be defined as permanent function, which is a link with the Real.

*Yajña* (m): Ritual sacrifice. For Tradition the entire manifestation is a sacrifice on the part of *Puruṣa* and, in order to reproduce on the individual plane that which *Puruṣa* accomplished in the cosmic order, the human entity should take inspiration from it.

*Yama* (n): Prohibitions. The first step or means (*aṅga*) in the *Rajayoga* of Patañjali. The prohibitions are: non-violence, non-appropriation, non-falseness, continence, non-possessiveness.

*Yoga* (m): The reintegration of the individual into the universal, of the relative (*jīva*) into the absolute (*ātman*). One of the six *darśana*, it represents the doctrine of Union, it is not only a philosophy but proposes operative means to attain Union.

*Yogaśāstra* (n): Instructions, teachings on *yoga*, *yoga* practice.

*Yogi* or *Yogin* (m): One who practices *yoga*, who is advanced in *yoga*, who has attained Union, i.e. who is reintegrated in the *ātman*.

RAPHAEL

Unity of Tradition

Having attained a synthesis of Knowledge (with which eclecticism or syncretism are not to be confused), Raphael aims at 'presenting' the Universal Tradition in its many Eastern and Western expressions. He has spent a substantial number of years writing and publishing books on spiritual experience, and his works include commentaries on the *Qabbālāh*, Hermeticism and Alchemy. He has also commented on and compared the Orphic Tradition with the works of Plato, Parmenides and Plotinus. Furthermore, Raphael is the author of several books on the pathway of non-duality (*Advaita*), which he has translated from the original Sanskrit, offering commentaries on a number of key Vedantic texts.

With reference to Platonism, Raphael has highlighted the fact that, if we were to draw a parallel between Śaṅkara's *Advaita Vedānta* and a Traditional Western Philosophical Vision, we could refer to the Vision presented by Plato. Drawing such a parallel does not imply a search for reciprocal influences, but rather it points to something of paramount importance: a sole Truth, inherent in the doctrines and teachings of several great thinkers who, although far apart in time and space, have reached similar and in some cases even identical conclusions.

One notices how Raphael writes from a metaphysical perspective in order to manifest and underscore the Unity of Tradition, under the metaphysical perspective. This does not mean that he is in opposition to a dualistic perspective, or to the various religious faiths, or 'points of view.'

A true embodied metaphysical Vision cannot be opposed to anything.

Written in the light of the Unity of Tradition, Raphael's works, calling on the reader's intuition, present precise points of correspondence between Eastern and Western Teachings. These points of reference are useful for those who want to approach a comparative doctrinal study and to enter the spirit of the Unity of Teaching.

For those who follow either an Eastern or a Western traditional line, these correspondences help us comprehend how the *Philosophia Perennis* (Universal Tradition), which has no history and has not been formulated by human minds as such, 'comprehends universal truths that do not belong to any people or any age.' It is merely for lack of 'comprehension' or of 'synthetic vision' that one particular Branch is considered the sole reliable one. Such a position can only lead to opposition and fanaticism. What can degenerate the Doctrine is either a sentimental, fanatical devotion or a condescending intellectualism that is critical and sterile, dogmatic and separative.

In Raphael's words: 'For those of us who aim at Realization, our task is to get to the essence of every Doctrine, because we know that just as Truth is one, so Tradition is one, even if, just like Truth, Tradition may be viewed from a plurality of apparently different points of view. We must abandon all disquisitions concerning the phenomenal process of becoming and move onto the plane of Being. In other words: we must have a Philosophy of Being as the foundation of our search and of our realization.'[1]

---

[1] See Raphael, *Tat tvam asi (That thou art):* The Path of Fire according to the *Asparśavāda* (New York: Aurea Vidyā, 2002).

Raphael interprets spiritual practice as a 'Path of Fire.' Here is what he writes: '...The 'Path of Fire' is the pathway each disciple follows in all branches of Tradition; it is the Way of Return. Therefore, it is not the particular teaching of an individual or a path parallel to the one and only Main Road... After all, every disciple follows his own 'Path of Fire', no matter which Branch of Tradition he belongs to.'

In Raphael's view, what is important is to express through living and being the truth that one has been able to contemplate. Thus, for each being, one's expression of thought and action must be coherent and in agreement with one's own specific *dharma*.

After more than forty years of teaching, both oral and written, Raphael is now dedicating himself only to those people who wish to be 'doers' rather than 'sayers', according to St. Paul's expression.

Raphael is connected with the *maṭha* founded by *Śrī Ādi* Śaṅkara at Śṛṅgeri and Kāñcīpuram as well as with the Rāmaṇa Āśram at Tiruvannamalai.

Founder of the Āśram Vidyā Order, he now dedicates himself entirely to spiritual practice. He lives in a hermitage connected to the *āśram* and devotes himself completely to a vow of silence.

* * *

May Raphael's Consciousness, expression of Unity of Tradition, guide and illumine along this Opus all those who donate their *mens informalis* (non-formal mind) to the attainment of the highest known Realization.

PUBLICATIONS

## Aurea Vidyā Collection

1. Raphael, ***The Threefold Pathway of Fire*** - Thoughts that Vibrate for an Alchemical, Ṁsthetical and Metaphysical Asceticism
ISBN 978-1-931406-00-0

2. Raphael, ***At the Source of Life*** - Questions and Answers concerning the Ultimate Reality
ISBN 978-1-931406-01-7

3. Raphael, ***Beyond the illusion of the ego*** - Synthesis of a Realizative Process
ISBN 978-1-931406-03-1

4. Raphael, ***Tat tvam asi*** (That thou art) - The Path of Fire According to the Asparśavāda
ISBN 978-1-931406-12-3

5. Gauḍapāda, ***Māṇḍūkyakārikā*** - The Metaphysical Path of *Vedānta**
ISBN 978-1-931406-04-8

6. Raphael, ***Orphism and the Initiatory Tradition***
ISBN 978-1-931406-05-5

7. Śaṅkara, ***Ātmabodha*** - Self-knowledge*
ISBN 978-1-931406-06-2

8. Raphael, ***Initiation into the Philosophy of Plato***
ISBN 978-1-931406-07-9

9. Śaṅkara, ***Vivekacūḍāmaṇi*** - The Crest-jewel of Discernment*
ISBN 978-1-931406-08-6

10. ***Dṛdṛśyaviveka*** - A philosophical investigation into the nature of the 'Seer' and the 'seen'*
ISBN 978-1-931406-09-3

11. Parmenides, ***On the Order of Nature*** (Περί φύσεος) - For a Philosophical Asceticism*
ISBN 978-1-931406-10-9

12. Raphael, ***The Science of Love*** - From the desire of the senses to the Intellect of Love
ISBN 978-1-931406-12-3

13. Vyāsa, ***Bhagavadgītā*** - The Celestial Song*
ISBN 978-1-931406-13-0

14. Raphael, ***The Pathway of Fire according to the Qabbālāh*** (Ehjeh 'Ašer 'Ehjeh) - I am That I am
ISBN 978-1-931406-14-7

15. Patañjali, ***The Regal Way to Realization*** (*Yogadarśana*)*
ISBN 978-1-931406-15-4

16. Raphael, ***Beyond Doubt*** - Approaches to Non-duality
ISBN 978-1-931406-16-1

17. Bādarāyaṇa: ***Brahmasūtra****
ISBN 978-1-931406-17-8

18. Śaṅkara, ***Aparokṣānubhūti*** - Self-Realization*
ISBN 978-1-931406-19-2

19. Raphael, ***The Pathway of Non-Duality*** - Advaitavāda
ISBN 978-1-931406-21-5

20. ***Five Upaniṣads**** - Īśa Kaivalya Sarvasāra Amṛtabindu Atharvaśira
ISBN 978-1-931406-26-0

Related Publications

Raphael, ***Essence and Purpose of Yoga*** - The Initiatory Pathways to the Transcendent
Element Books, Shaftesbury, U.K
ISBN 978-1-852308-66-7

Biography, ***Śaṅkara***.
Aurea Vidyā, New York
ISBN 978-1-931406-11-6

Forthcoming Publications

Śaṅkara, ***Brief Works**** Treatises and Hymns

Raphael, ***Awakening***

***Upaniṣads**** by Raphael

* Translation from Sanskrit or Greek, and Commentary by Raphael.

Aurea Vidyā is the Publishing House of the Parmenides Traditional Philosophy Foundation, a Not-for-Profit Organization whose purpose is to make Perennial Philosophy accessible.

The Foundation goes about its purpose in a number of ways: by publishing and distributing Traditional Philosophy texts with Aurea Vidyā, by offering individual and group encounters, by providing a Reading Room and daily Meditations, at its Center.

* * *

Those readers who have an interest in Traditional Philosophy are welcome to contact the Foundation at: parmenides.foundation@earthlink.net.

www.ingramcontent.com/pod-product-compliance
Lightning Source LLC
Chambersburg PA
CBHW030234170426
43201CB00006B/211
*9781931406260*